Poems for All
Occasions

Publisher and Creative Director: Nick Wells
Project Editor: Chelsea Edwards
Art Director and Layout Design: Mike Spender
Digital Design and Production: Chris Herbert
Proofreader: Dawn Laker

Special thanks to: Catherine Taylor and Aly Dixon

FLAME TREE PUBLISHING
Crabtree Hall, Crabtree Lane
Fulham, London, SW6 6TY
United Kingdom

www.flametreepublishing.com

First published 2010

10 12 14 13 11
1 3 5 7 9 10 8 6 4 2

Flame Tree is part of The Foundry Creative Media Company Limited

© 2010 Flame Tree Publishing

ISBN 978 1 84786 709 4

Printed in China

Poems for All
Occasions

FLAME TREE
PUBLISHING

Contents

Introduction

Poetry has existed throughout time as an artistic and poignant form of communication. It is the ultimate expression of emotion and there are no defined rules governing its content. Poetry can convey some of our most complex emotions and at times expresses what we cannot find the words to say. This quality has led to poems being used for all manner of social occasions to verbalize our innermost thoughts. This new collection of poetry encompasses a variety

of topics on which you may look to poetry for inspiration. Whether you are welcoming a child into the world or wishing one well as they leave university, or sharing your feelings of love on your wedding day or Valentine's, then you will undoubtedly find a poem to satisfy your needs.

The birth of a child is one of the greatest gifts in life and is often cause for poetic revelation. In 'To a Young Mother on the Birth of Her First Born Child,' Rosanna Eleanor Leprohon (1829–79) speaks of the importance of God in an infant's life. The celebration of a child through their Christening is an undeniable source of joy for many parents and is thus an institution worthy of poetic consideration.

Love as a subject of poetry is unquestionably abundant and the occasion of a wedding is a chance to celebrate the most acclaimed of romantic poems. Including Elizabeth Barrett Browning's (1806–61) 'How Do I Love Thee?' along with Shakespeare's 'Sonnet 116', this chapter exhibits the most heartfelt of lines to treasure during any celebration of love.

There are also some holidays that are excellent candidates for inclusion in a collection such as this one. Religious celebrations such as Easter and Christmas alongside more secular days of observance such as Mother's Day and Valentine's Day are common provocations of poetic composition. As an opportunity to give thanks, blessings or to simply translate feelings of love into eloquent language, this selection includes the festive sentiments of Louisa May Alcott's (1832–88) 'From Our Happy Home' to the romantic utterances of Robert Burns's (1759–96) 'A Red, Red Rose.'

Along with celebrating times of happiness and festivity, poetry is invaluable when it comes to honouring loved ones we have lost. Perhaps you are looking for a poem to read at a funeral or just hoping to find something that will go a small way to helping you cope. Hopefully you will find some comfort in 'Eulogy for a Veteran' or Anne Brontë's (1820–49) 'Farewell'.

Organized into four chapters, this collection demonstrates how poetry can provide an outlet for the multitude of reactions to treasured holidays and life events. Through birth, religious celebration and memorial, tragedy, love and loss, it has endured as one of the most valuable and comforting forms of literature.

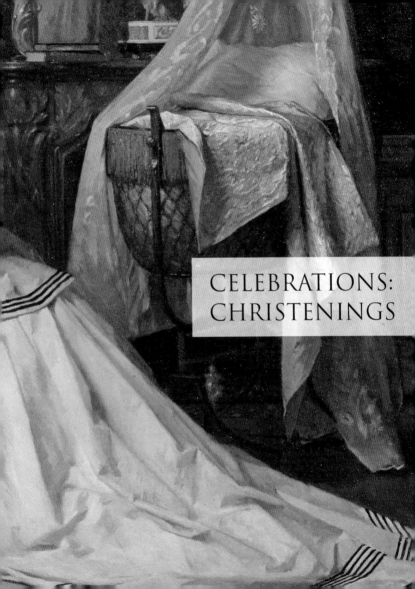

CELEBRATIONS: CHRISTENINGS

Monday's child is fair of face,
Tuesday's child is full of grace,
Wednesday's child is full of woe,
Thursday's child has far to go,
Friday's child is loving and giving,
Saturday's child works hard for a living,
But the child that is born on the Sabbath day,
Is merry, and happy, and bright, and gay.

English Proverb

Infant Joy

I have no name
I am but two days old. –
What shall I call thee?
I happy am
Joy is my name, –
Sweet joy befall thee!

Pretty joy!
Sweet joy but two days old.
Sweet joy I call thee:
Thou dost smile.
I sing the while
Sweet joy befall thee.

William Blake (1757–1827)

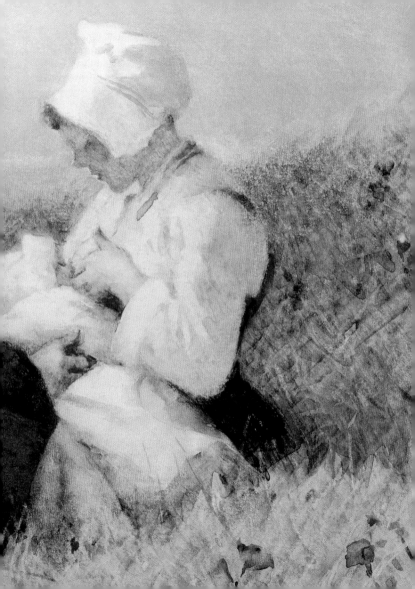

'Tell me, tell me, smiling child'

Tell me, tell me, smiling child,
What the past is like to thee?
An Autumn evening soft and mild
With a wind that sighs mournfully.

Tell me what is the present hour?
A green and flowery spray
Where a young bird sits gathering its power
To mount and fly away.

And what is the future, happy one?
A sea beneath a cloudless sun,
A mighty glorious dazzling sea
Stretching into infinity.

Emily Brontë (1818–48)

I Know A Baby, Such A Baby

I know a baby, such a baby, –
Round blue eyes and cheeks of pink,
Such an elbow furrowed with dimples,
Such a wrist where creases sink.
Cuddle and love me, cuddle and love me,
Crows the mouth of coral pink:
Oh, the bald head, and, oh, the sweet lips,
And, oh, the sleepy eyes that wink!

Christina Georgina Rossetti (1830–94)

Babyhood

I.

A baby shines as bright
If winter or if May be
On eyes that keep in sight
    A baby.

Though dark the skies or grey be,
It fills our eyes with light,
If midnight or midday be.

Love hails it, day and night,
The sweetest thing that may be
Yet cannot praise aright
    A baby.

II.

All heaven, in every baby born,
All absolute of earthly leaven,
Reveals itself, though man may scorn
   All heaven.

Yet man might feel all sin forgiven,
All grief appeased, all pain outworn,
By this one revelation given.

Soul, now forget thy burdens borne:
Heart, be thy joys now seven times seven:
Love shows in light more bright than morn
   All heaven.

III.

What likeness may define, and stray not
    From truth's exactest way,
A baby's beauty? Love can say not
    What likeness may.

The Mayflower loveliest held in May
    Of all that shine and stay not
Laughs not in rosier disarray.

Sleek satin, swansdown, buds that play not
    As yet with winds that play,
Would fain be matched with this, and may not:
    What likeness may?

IV.

Rose, round whose bed
Dawn's cloudlets close,
Earth's brightest-bred
   Rose!

No song, love knows,
May praise the head
Your curtain shows.

Ere sleep has fled,
The whole child glows
One sweet live red
   Rose.

Algernon Charles Swinburne (1837–1909)

Choosing A Name

I have got a new-born sister;
I was nigh the first that kissed her.
When the nursing woman brought her
To papa, his infant daughter,
How papa's dear eyes did glisten! –
She will shortly be to christen:
And papa has made the offer,
I shall have the naming of her.

Now I wonder what would please her,
Charlotte, Julia, or Louisa.
Ann and Mary, they're too common;
Joan's too formal for a woman;
Jane's a prettier name beside;
But we had a Jane that died.
They would say, if 'twas Rebecca,
That she was a little Quaker.
Edith's pretty, but that looks
Better in old English books;
Ellen's left off long ago;
Blanche is out of fashion now.

None that I have named as yet
Are so good as Margaret.
Emily is neat and fine.
What do you think of Caroline?
How I'm puzzled and perplext
What to choose or think of next!
I am in a little fever.
Lest the name that I shall give her
Should disgrace her or defame her,
I will leave papa to name her.

Charles Lamb (1775–1834)

Lullaby

Sleep, little baby, sleep, love, sleep!
Evening is coming, and night is nigh;
Under the lattice the little birds cheep,
All will be sleeping by and by.
Sleep, little baby, sleep.

Sleep, little baby, sleep, love, sleep!
Darkness is creeping along the sky;
Stars at the casement glimmer and peep,
Slowly the moon comes sailing by.
Sleep, little baby, sleep.

Sleep, little baby, sleep, love, sleep!
Sleep till the dawning has dappled the sky;
Under the lattice the little birds cheep,
All will be waking by and by.
Sleep, little baby, sleep.

Horace Smith (1779–1849)

Baby

Where did you come from, baby dear?
Out of the everywhere into here.

Where did you get those eyes so blue?
Out of the sky as I came through.

What makes the light in them sparkle and spin?
Some of the starry twinkles left in.

Where did you get that little tear?
I found it waiting when I got here.

What makes your forehead so smooth and high?
A soft hand stroked it as I went by.

What makes your cheek like a warm white rose?
I saw something better than anyone knows.

Whence that three-cornered smile of bliss?
Three angels gave me at once a kiss.

Where did you get this pearly ear?
God spoke, and it came out to hear.

Where did you get those arms and hands?
Love made itself into bonds and bands.

Feet, whence did you come, you darling things?
From the same box as the cherubs' wings.

How did they all just come to be you?
God thought about me, and so I grew.

But how did you come to us, you dear?
God thought about you, and so I am here.

George MacDonald (1824–1905)

The Mother's Hope

Is there, when the winds are singing
In the happy summer time, –
When the raptured air is ringing
With Earth's music heavenward springing

Forest chirp, and village chime, –
Is there, of the sounds that float
Unsighingly, a single note
Half so sweet, and clear, and wild,
As the laughter of a child?

Listen! and be now delighted:
Morn hath touched her golden strings;
Earth and Sky their vows have plighted;
Life and Light are reunited

Amid countless carollings;
Yet, delicious as they are,
There's a sound that's sweeter far, –
One that makes the heart rejoice
More than all, – the human voice!

Organ finer, deeper, clearer,
Though it be a stranger's tone, –
Than the winds or waters dearer,
More enchanting to the hearer,

For it answereth to his own.
But, of all its witching words,
Those are sweetest, bubbling wild
Through the laugher of a child.

Harmonies from time-touched towers,
Haunted strains from rivulets,
Hum of bees among the flowers,
Rustling leaves, and silver showers, –

These, erelong, the ear forgets;
But in mine there is a sound
Ringing on the whole year round, –
Heart-deep laughter that I heard
Ere my child could speak a word.

Ah! 'twas heard by ear far purer,
Fondlier formed to catch the strain, –
Ear of one whose love is surer, –
Hers, the mother, the endurer

Of the deepest share of pain;
Here the deepest bliss to treasure
Memories of that cry of pleasure;
Hers to hoard, a lifetime after,
Echoes of that infant laughter.

'Tis a mother's large affection
Hears with a mysterious sense, –
Breathings that evade detection,
Whisper faint, and fine inflection,

Thrill in her with power intense.
Childhood's honeyed words untaught
Hiveth she in loving thought, –
Tones that never thence depart;
For she listens – with her heart.

Samuel Laman Blanchard (1803–45)

An Extract from Evening Song of the Thoughtful Child

Shadow children, thin and small,
Now the day is left behind,
You are dancing on the wall,
On the curtains, on the blind.

On the ceiling, children, too,
Peeping round the nursery door,
Let me come and play with you,
As we always played before.

Let's pretend that we have wings
And can really truly fly
Over every sort of things
Up and up into the sky.

Katherine Mansfield (1888–1923)

To a Young Mother on the Birth of Her First Born Child

Young mother! proudly throbs thine heart, and
    well may it rejoice,
Well may'st thou raise to Heaven above in grateful
    prayer thy voice:
A gift hath been bestowed on thee, a gift of
    priceless worth,
Far dearer to thy woman's heart than all the
    wealth of earth.

What store of deep and holy joy is opened to thy thought –
Glad, sunny dreams of future days, with bliss
    and rapture fraught;
Of hopes as varied, yet as bright, as beams of April sun,
And plans and wishes centred all within thy darling one!

While others seek in changing scenes earth's
    happiness to gain,
In fashion's halls to win a joy as dazzling as 'tis vain –
A bliss more holy far is thine, far sweeter and more deep,
To watch beside thine infant's couch and bend
    above his sleep.

What joy for thee to ling'ring gaze within
    those cloudless eyes,
Turning upon thee with a glance of such sweet,
    strange surprise,
Or press a mother's loving kiss upon that fair, white brow,
Of all earth's weight of sin and care and pain
    unconscious now.

Then, as thy loved one's sleeping breath so softly
   fans thy cheek,
And gazing on that tiny form, so lovely, yet so weak,
A dream comes o'er thee of the time when nobly at thy side
Thy cherished son shall proudly stand, in manhood's
   lofty pride.

Yet a sad change steals slowly o'er thy tender, loving eye,
Thou twin'st him closer to thy heart, with fond and
   anxious sigh,
Feeling, however bright his course he too must
   suff'ring know,
Like all earth's children taste alike life's cup of
   care and woe.

But, oh! it lies within thy power to give to him a spell
To guard him in the darkest hour from sorrow safe and well;
Thou'lt find it in the narrow path the great and good
   have trod –
And thou thyself wilt teach it him—the knowledge
   of his God!

Rosanna Eleanor Leprohon (1829–79)

The Stork

Last night the Stork came stalking,
And, Stork, beneath your wing
Lay, lapped in dreamless slumber,
The tiniest little thing!
From Babyland, out yonder
Beside a silver sea,
You brought a priceless treasure
As gift to mine and me!

Last night my dear one listened –
And, wife, you knew the cry –
The dear old Stork has sought our home
A many times gone by!
And in your gentle bosom
I found the pretty thing
That from the realm out yonder
Our friend the Stork did bring.

Last night a babe awakened,
And, babe, how strange and new
Must seem the home and people
The Stork has brought you to;
And yet methinks you like them –
You neither stare nor weep,
But closer to my dear one
You cuddle, and you sleep!

Last night my heart grew fonder –
O happy heart of mine,
Sing of the inspirations
That round my pathway shine!
And sing your sweetest love-song
To this dear nestling wee
The Stork from 'Way-Out-Yonder'
Hath brought to mine and me!

Eugene Field (1850–95)

Cradle Song

Sweet dreams form a shade,
O'er my lovely infant's head.
Sweet dreams of pleasant streams,
By happy silent moony beams

Sweet sleep with soft down.
Weave thy brows an infant crown.
Sweet sleep Angel mild,
Hover o'er my happy child.

Sweet smiles in the night,
Hover over my delight.
Sweet smiles Mother's smiles,
All the livelong night beguiles.

Sweet moans, dovelike sighs,
Chase not slumber from thy eyes,
Sweet moans, sweeter smiles,
All the dovelike moans beguiles.

Sleep sleep happy child,
All creation slept and smil'd.
Sleep sleep, happy sleep.
While o'er thee thy Mother weep

Sweet babe in thy face,
Holy image I can trace.
Sweet babe once like thee,
Thy maker lay and wept for me

Wept for me for thee for all,
When he was an infant small.
Thou his image ever see.
Heavenly face that smiles on thee,

Smiles on thee on me on all,
Who became an infant small,
Infant smiles are His own smiles,
Heaven and earth to peace beguiles.

William Blake (1757–1827)

Baby May

CHEEKS as soft as July peaches,
Lips whose dewy scarlet teaches
Poppies paleness – round large eyes
Ever great with new surprise,
Minutes fill'd with shadeless gladness,
Minutes just as brimm'd with sadness,
Happy smiles and wailing cries,
Crows and laughs and tearful eyes,
Lights and shadows swifter born
Than on wind-swept Autumn corn,
Ever some new tiny notion
Making every limb all motion –
Catching up of legs and arms,
Throwings back and small alarms,
Clutching fingers – straightening jerks,
Twining feet whose each toe works,
Kickings up and straining risings,
Mother's ever new surprisings,
Hands all wants and looks all wonder
At all things the heavens under,
Tiny scorns of smil'd reprovings
That have more of love than lovings,
Mischiefs done with such a winning
Archness, that we prize such sinning,
Breakings dire of plates and glasses,
Graspings small at all that passes,
Pullings off of all that's able
To be caught from tray or table;

Silences – small meditations,
Deep as thoughts of cares for nations,
Breaking into wisest speeches,
In a tongue that nothing teaches,
All the thoughts of whose possessing
Must be wooed to light by guessing;
Slumbers – such sweet angel-seemings,
That we'd ever have such dreamings,
Till from sleep we see thee breaking,
And we'd always have thee waking;
Wealth for which we know no measure,
Pleasure high above all pleasure,
Gladness brimming over gladness,
Joy in care – delight in sadness,
Loveliness beyond completeness,
Sweetness distancing all sweetness,
Beauty all that beauty may be –
That's May Bennett, that's my baby.

William Cox Bennett (1820–95)

CELEBRATIONS:
GRADUATION

If...

If you can keep your head when all about you
    Are losing theirs and blaming it on you;
If you can trust yourself when all men doubt you,
    But make allowance for their doubting too:
If you can wait and not be tired by waiting,
    Or, being lied about, don't deal in lies,
Or being hated don't give way to hating,
    And yet don't look too good, nor talk too wise;

If you can dream – and not make dreams your master;
    If you can think – and not make thoughts your aim,
If you can meet with Triumph and Disaster
    And treat those two impostors just the same:
If you can bear to hear the truth you've spoken
    Twisted by knaves to make a trap for fools,
Or watch the things you gave your life to, broken,
    And stoop and build'em up with worn-out tools;

If you can make one heap of all your winnings
    And risk it on one turn of pitch-and-toss,
And lose, and start again at your beginnings,
    And never breathe a word about your loss:
If you can force your heart and nerve and sinew
    To serve your turn long after they are gone,
And so hold on when there is nothing in you
    Except the Will which says to them: 'Hold on!'

If you can talk with crowds and keep your virtue,
 Or walk with Kings – nor lose the common touch,
If neither foes nor loving friends can hurt you,
 If all men count with you, but none too much:
If you can fill the unforgiving minute
 With sixty seconds' worth of distance run,
Yours is the Earth and everything that's in it,
 And which is more; you'll be a Man, my son!

Rudyard Kipling (1865–1936)

Life

All in the dark we grope along,
And if we go amiss
We learn at least which path is wrong,
And there is gain in this.

We do not always win the race,
By only running right,
We have to tread the mountain's base
Before we reach its height.

The Christs alone no errors made;
So often had they trod
The paths that led through light and shade,
They had become as God.

As Krishna, Buddha, Christ again,
They passed along the way,
And left those mighty truths which men
But dimly grasp to-day.

But he who loves himself the last
And knows the use of pain,
Though strewn with errors all his past,
He surely shall attain.

Some souls there are that needs must taste
Of wrong, ere choosing right;
We should not call those years a waste
Which led us to the light.

Ella Wheeler Wilcox (1850–1919)

One of These Days

Say! Let's forget it! Let's put it aside!
Life is so large and the world is so wide.
Days are so short and there's so much to do,
What if it was false – there's plenty that's true.
Say! Let's forget it! Let's brush it away
Now and forever, so what do you say?
All of the bitter words said may be praise
One of these days.

Say! Let's forget it! Let's wipe off the slate,
Find something better to cherish than hate.
There's so much good in the world that we've had,
Let's strike a balance and cross off the bad.
Say! Let's forgive it, whatever it be,
Let's not be slaves when we ought to be free.
We shall be walking in sunshiny ways
One of these days.

Say! Let's not mind it! Let's smile it away,
Bring not a withered rose from yesterday;
Flowers are so fresh from the wayside and wood,
Sorrows are blessings but half understood.
Say! Let's not mind it, however it seems,
Hope is so sweet and holds so many dreams;
All of the sere fields with blossoms shall blaze
One of these days.

Say! Let's not take it so sorely to heart!
Hates may be friendships just drifted apart,
Failure be genius not quite understood,
Say! Let's get closer to somebody's side,
See what his dreams are and learn how he tried,
See if our scoldings won't give way to praise
One of these days.

Say! Let's not wither! Let's branch out and rise
Out of the byways and nearer the skies.
Let's spread some shade that's refreshing and deep
Where some tired traveler may lie down and sleep.
Say! Let's not tarry! Let's do it right now;
So much to do if we just find out how!
We may not be here to help folks or praise
One of these days.

James W. Foley (1874–1939)

Wishing

Do you wish the world were better?
Let me tell you what to do.
Set a watch upon your actions,
Keep them always straight and true.
Rid your mind of selfish motives,
Let your thoughts be clean and high.
You can make a little Eden
Of the sphere you occupy.

Do you wish the world were wiser?
Well, suppose you make a start,
By accumulating wisdom
In the scrapbook of your heart;
Do not waste one page on folly;
Live to learn, and learn to live
If you want to give men knowledge
You must get, ere you give.

Do you wish the world were happy?
Then remember day by day
Just to scatter seeds of kindness
As you pass along the way,
For the pleasures of the many
May be ofttimes traced to one,
As the hand that plants an acorn
Shelters armies from the sun.

Ella Wheeler Wilcox (1850–1919)

Four Things

Four things a man must learn to do
If he would make his record true:
To think without confusion clearly;
To love his fellow man sincerely;
To act from honest motives purely;
To trust in God and Heaven securely.

Henry Van Dyke (1852–1933)

The Graduate Leaving College

What summons do I hear?
The morning peal, departure's knell;
My eyes let fall a friendly tear,
And bid this place farewell.

Attending servants come,
The carriage wheels like thunders roar,
To bear the pensive seniors home,
Here to be seen no more.

Pass one more transient night,
The morning sweeps the college clean;
The graduate takes his last long flight,
No more in college seen.

The bee, which courts the flower,
Must with some pain itself employ,
And then fly, at the day's last hour,
Home to its hive with joy.

George Moses Horton (1779–1883)

Do Your Best and Leave the Rest

As through life you journey onward
   Many a hill you'll have to climb;
Many a rough and dang'rous pathway,
   You'll encounter time and time.
Now and then a gleam of sunshine,
   Will bring hope to cheer your breast;
Then press onward, – ever trusting, –
   Do your best and leave the rest.

Though your progress may be hindered,
   By false friends or bitter foes;
And the goal for which you're striving,
   Seems so far away, – who knows?
You may yet have strength to reach it,
   E'er the sun sinks in the west;
Ever striving, – still undaunted;
   Do your best and leave the rest.

If you fail, as thousands must do,
   You will still have cause for pride;
You will have advanced much further,
   Than if you had never tried.
Never falter, but remember,
   Life is not a foolish jest;
You all are in the fight to win it;
   Do your best and leave the rest.

If at last your strength shall fail you,
    And your struggles have proved vain;
There is One who will sustain you;
    Soothe your sorrow, – ease your pain,
He has seen your earnest striving,
    And your efforts shall be blest;
For He knows that you, though failing,
    Did your best, – He'll do the rest.

John Hartley (1839–1917)

CELEBRATIONS:
ANNIVERSARIES

Extract from An Anniversary

AS flower to sun its drop of dew
    Gives from its crystal cup,
So I, as morning gift to you,
    This poor verse offer up.

As flowers upon the summer wind
    Their airborne odours shake,
So, in all fragrance you may find,
    I give but what I take.

My tree blooms green through snow and heat;
    Your love is sap and root, –
And this is but the breathing sweet
    Of fairest blossom-shoot.

An outgrowth of the happy days
    In wedded lives begun –
Two lives, in all their work and ways,
    Indissolubly one.

The force that was to bind us so
    We very dimly knew.
Ah, love! it seems so long ago,
    And yet the years are few.

We did not wait for tides to rise,
    Nor cared that winds were rough;
They call'd us foolish – we were wise;
    God gave us wealth enough.

He only knows what precious change
    We took of Him for gold;
What blessing such a narrow range
    Of circumstance can hold.

No troubles now could memory spare,
    No lightest touch of pain;
No hand experience of care
    Would we unlearn again.

Such love surrounds, such beauty lies
    On our most common needs,
As silver hoar-frost glorifies
    The wayside sticks and weeds.

All trials that are overpast,
    All cares that are to be,
But make more sacred and more fast
    The ties 'twixt you and me.

They are but clear lights shining through
    The mist that round us rolls;
They are but touchstones, fine and true
    For fond and faithful souls.

They are but fires, to cleanse and clean
    Our human love from stain;
For naught of sordid, false, or mean
    From these blest fires remain.

They are but keys within the wards
    Of that last, inmost door,
Where the heart's dearest treasure-hoards
    Are garner'd evermore.

Ah, dear! our very griefs are glad
    Our every cross is crown'd;
We are not able to be sad,
    Such comfort wraps us round.

How calm the haven where we rest,
    Now passion's storms are past!
How warm and soft the little nest
    Which shelters us at last!

How – blue, pellucid, and divine –
    Through all our days and nights,
The clear eyes of our children shine
    Like heavenly beacon-lights!

Ada Cambridge (1844–1926)

My True-Love Hath my Heart, and I Have His

My true-love hath my heart, and I have his,
By just exchange, one for the other giv'n.
I hold his dear, and mine he cannot miss;
There never was a better bargain driv'n.
His heart in me keeps me and him in one,
My heart in him his thoughts and senses guides;
He loves my heart, for once it was his own;
I cherish his, because in me it bides.
His heart his wound received from my sight:
My heart was wounded with his wounded heart;
For as from me, on him his hurt did light,
So still me thought in me his hurt did smart:
Both equal hurt, in this change sought our bliss:
My true-love hath my heart and I have his.

Sir Philip Sidney (1554–86)

To My Dear Loving Husband

If ever two were one, then surely we.
If ever man were loved by wife, then thee;
If ever wife was happy in a man,
Compare with me, ye woman, if you can.
I prize thy love more than whole mines of gold
Or all the riches that the East doth hold.
My love is such that rivers cannot quench,
Nor ought but love from thee, give recompense.
Thy love is such I can no way repay,
The heavens reward thee manifold, I pray.
The while we live, in love let's so persevere,
That when we live no more, we may live ever.

Anne Bradstreet (1612–72)

The Presence of Love

And in Life's noisiest hour,
There whispers still the ceaseless Love of Thee,
The heart's Self-solace and soliloquy.

You mould my Hopes, you fashion me within;
And to the leading Love-throb in the Heart
Thro' all my Being, thro' my pulses beat;
You lie in all my many Thoughts, like Light,
Like the fair light of Dawn, or summer Eve
On rippling Stream, or cloud-reflecting Lake.
And looking to the Heaven, that bends above you,
How oft! I bless the Lot, that made me love you.

Samuel Taylor Coleridge (1772–1834)

I Love Thee

I love thee, as I love the calm
Of sweet, star-lighted hours!
I love thee, as I love the balm
Of early jes'mine flow'rs.
I love thee, as I love the last
Rich smile of fading day,
Which lingereth, like the look we cast,
On rapture pass'd away.
I love thee as I love the tone
Of some soft-breathing flute
Whose soul is wak'd for me alone,
When all beside is mute.

I love thee as I love the first
Young violet of the spring;
Or the pale lily, April-nurs'd,
To scented blossoming.
I love thee, as I love the full,
Clear gushings of the song,
Which lonely – sad – and beautiful –
At night-fall floats along,
Pour'd by the bulbul forth to greet
The hours of rest and dew;
When melody and moonlight meet
To blend their charm, and hue.
I love thee, as the glad bird loves
The freedom of its wing,
On which delightedly it moves
In wildest wandering.

I love thee as I love the swell,
And hush, of some low strain,
Which bringeth, by its gentle spell,
The past to life again.
Such is the feeling which from thee
Nought earthly can allure:
'Tis ever link'd to all I see
Of gifted – high – and pure!

Eliza Acton (1799–1859)

CELEBRATIONS:
BURNS NIGHT

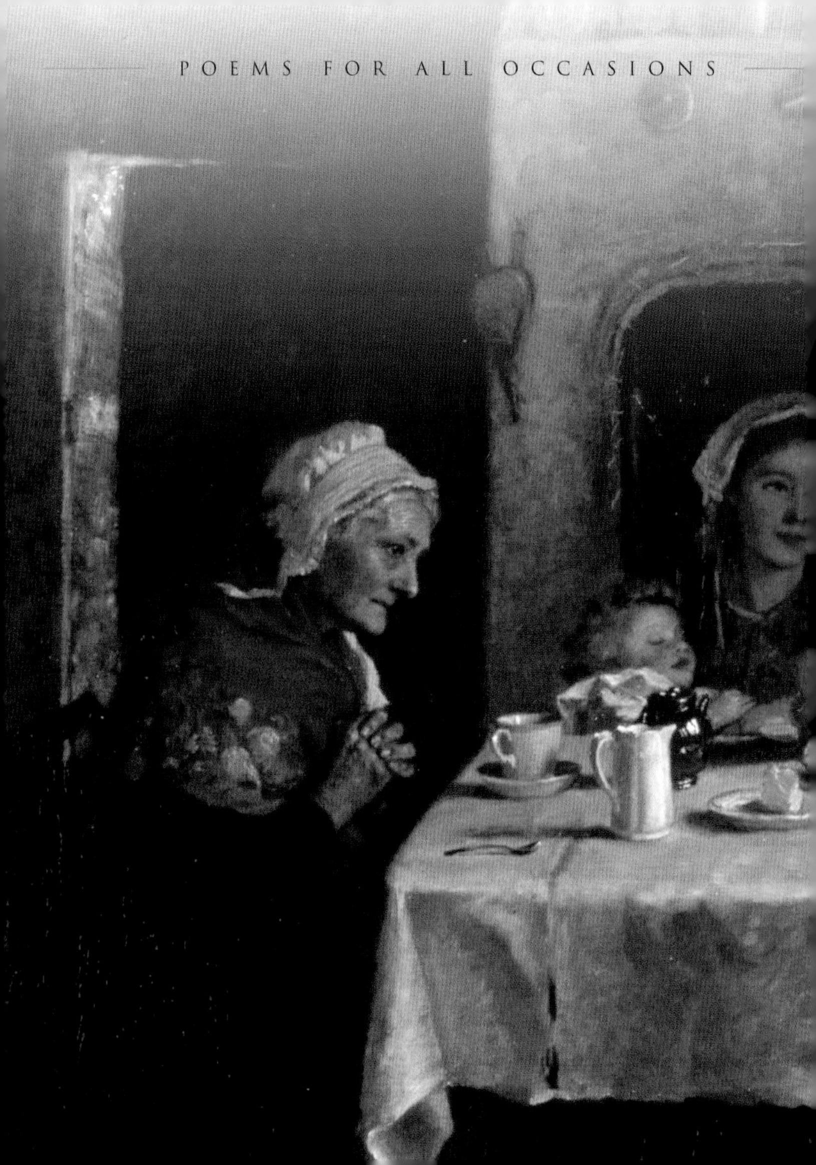

The Selkirk Grace

Some hae meat and canna eat,
And some wad eat that want it,
But we hae meat and we can eat,
And sae the Lord be thankit.

Author Unknown, but often wrongly
attributed to Robert Burns

Address to a Haggis

Fair fa' your honest, sonsie face,
Great chieftain o' the pudding-race!
Aboon them a' ye tak your place,
Painch, tripe, or thairm :
Weel are ye wordy o'a grace
As lang's my arm.

The groaning trencher there ye fill,
Your hurdies like a distant hill,
Your pin wad help to mend a mill
In time o'need,
While thro' your pores the dews distil
Like amber bead.

His knife see rustic Labour dight,
An' cut you up wi' ready sleight,
Trenching your gushing entrails bright,
Like ony ditch;
And then, O what a glorious sight,
Warm-reekin', rich!

Then, horn for horn, they stretch an' strive:
Deil tak the hindmost! on they drive,
Till a' their weel-swall'd kytes belyve
Are bent like drums;
Then auld Guidman, maist like to rive,
Bethankit! hums.

Is there that owre his French ragout
Or olio that wad staw a sow,
Or fricassee wad make her spew
Wi' perfect sconner,
Looks down wi' sneering, scornfu' view
On sic a dinner?

Poor devil! see him owre his trash,
As feckless as wither'd rash,
His spindle shank, a guid whip-lash;
His nieve a nit;
Thro' bloody flood or field to dash,
O how unfit!

But mark the Rustic, haggis-fed,
The trembling earth resounds his tread.
Clap in his walie nieve a blade,
He'll mak it whissle;
An' legs an' arms, an' heads will sned,
Like taps o' thrissle.

Ye Pow'rs, wha mak mankind your care,
And dish them out their bill o' fare,
Auld Scotland wants nae skinking ware
That jaups in luggies;
But, if ye wish her gratefu' prayer
Gie her a haggis!

Robert Burns (1759–96)

My Bonnie Bell

The smiling Spring comes in rejoicing,
And surly Winter grimly flies;
Now crystal clear are the falling waters,
And bonnie blue are the sunny skies.
Fresh o'er the mountains breaks forth the morning,
The ev'ning gilds the ocean's swell;
All creatures joy in the sun's returning,
And I rejoice in my bonnie Bell.

The flowery Spring leads sunny Summer,
The yellow Autumn presses near;
Then in his turn comes gloomy Winter,
Till smiling Spring again appear:
Thus seasons dancing, life advancing,
Old Time and Nature their changes tell;
But never ranging, still unchanging,
I adore my bonnie Bell.

Robert Burns (1759–96)

To A Louse

Ha! whaur ye gaun, ye crowlin ferlie?
Your impudence protects you sairly;
I canna say but ye strunt rarely,
Owre gauze and lace;
Tho', faith! I fear ye dine but sparely
On sic a place.

Ye ugly, creepin, blastit wonner,
Detested, shunn'd by saunt an' sinner,
How daur ye set your fit upon her –
Sae fine a lady?
Gae somewhere else and seek your dinner
On some poor body.

Swith! in some beggar's haffet squattle;
There ye may creep, and sprawl, and sprattle,
Wi' ither kindred, jumping cattle,
In shoals and nations;
Whaur horn nor bane ne'er daur unsettle
Your thick plantations.

Now haud you there, ye're out o' sight,
Below the fatt'rels, snug and tight;
Na, faith ye yet! ye'll no be right,
Till ye've got on it –
The verra tapmost, tow'rin height
O' Miss' bonnet.

My sooth! right bauld ye set your nose out,
As plump an' grey as ony groset:
O for some rank, mercurial rozet,
Or fell, red smeddum,
I'd gie you sic a hearty dose o't,
Wad dress your droddum.

I wad na been surpris'd to spy
You on an auld wife's flainen toy;
Or aiblins some bit dubbie boy,
On's wyliecoat;
But Miss' fine Lunardi! fye!
How daur ye do't?

O Jenny, dinna toss your head,
An' set your beauties a' abroad!
Ye little ken what cursed speed
The blastie's makin:
Thae winks an' finger-ends, I dread,
Are notice takin.

O wad some Power the giftie gie us
To see oursels as ithers see us!
It wad frae mony a blunder free us,
An' foolish notion:
What airs in dress an' gait wad lea'e us,
An' ev'n devotion!

Robert Burns (1759–96)

Auld Lang Syne

Should auld acquaintance be forgot,
And never brought to mind?
Should auld acquaintance be forgot,
And auld lang syne!

For auld lang syne, my jo,
For auld lang syne,
We'll tak a cup o' kindness yet,
For auld lang syne.

And surely ye'll be your pint stowp!
And surely I'll be mine!
And we'll tak a cup o' kindness yet,
For auld lang syne.

We twa hae run about the braes,
And pou'd the gowan fine;
But we've wander'd mony a weary fitt,
Sin' auld lang syne.

We twa hae paidl'd in the burn,
Frae morning sun till dine;
But seas between us braid hae roar'd
Sin' auld lang syne.

And there's a hand, my trusty fiere!
And gie's a hand o' thine!
And we'll tak a right gude-willie-waught,
For auld lang syne.

For auld lang syne, my jo,
For auld lang syne,
We'll tak a cup o' kindness yet,
For auld lang syne.

Robert Burns (1759–96)

WEDDINGS

1 Corinthians 13: 4-8

Love is patient, Love is kind,
It does not envy, it does not boast,
It is not proud, it is not rude,
It is not self-seeking,
It is not easily angered,
It keeps no record of wrongs.
Love does not delight in evil,
but rejoices with the truth.
Love always protects, always trusts,
always hopes, always perseveres.
Love bears all things, believes all things,
hopes all things, endures all things.
Love never ends.

How Do I Love Thee?

How do I love thee? Let me count the ways.
I love thee to the depth and breadth and height
My soul can reach, when feeling out of sight
For the ends of Being an Ideal Grace.
I love thee to the level of every day's
Most quiet need, by sun and candle-light.
I love thee freely, as men strive for Right;
I love thee purely, as they turn from Praise.
I love thee with the passion put to use
In my old grief's, and with my childhood's faith.
I love thee with a love I seemed to lose
With my lost saints, I love thee with the breath,
Smiles, tears, of all my life! and, if God choose,
I shall but love thee better after death.

Elizabeth Barrett Browning (1806–61)

Believe Me, If All Those Endearing Young Charms

Believe me, if all those endearing young charms,
Which I gaze on so fondly to-day,
Were to change by to-morrow, and fleet in my arms,
Live fairy-gifts fading away,
Thou wouldst still be adored, as this moment thou art,
Let thy loveliness fade as it will,
And around the dear ruin each wish of my heart
Would entwine itself verdantly still.

It is not while beauty and youth are thine own,
And thy cheeks unprofaned by a tear,
That the fervour and faith of a soul may be known,
To which time will but make thee more dear!
No, the heart that has truly loved never forgets,
But as truly loves on to the close,
As the sunflower turns on her god when he sets
The same look which she turned when he rose!

Thomas Moore (1779–1852)

Sonnet 116

Let me not to the marriage of true minds
Admit impediments. Love is not love
Which alters when it alteration finds,
Or bends with the remover to remove.
O, no! it is an ever-fixed mark,
That looks on tempests and is never shaken;
It is the star to every wand'ring bark,
Whose worth's unknown, although his height be taken.
Love's not Time's fool, though rosy lips and cheeks
Within his bending sickle's compass come;
Love alters not with his brief hours and weeks,
But bears it out even to the edge of doom.
    If this be error, and upon me prov'd
    I never writ, nor no man ever lov'd.

William Shakespeare (1564–1616)

Of Pearls and Stars

The pearly treasures of the sea,
The lights that spatter heaven above,
More precious than these wonders are
My heart-of-hearts filled with your love.

The ocean's power, the heavenly sights
Cannot outweigh a love-filled heart.
And sparkling stars or glowing pearls
Pale as love flashes, beams and darts.

So, little, youthful maiden come
Into my ample, feverish heart
For heaven and earth and sea and sky
Do melt as love has melt my heart.

Heinrich Heine (1797–1856)

The Passionate Shepherd to His Love

Come live with me and be my love,
And we will all the pleasures prove,
That valleys, groves, hills and fields,
Woods or steepy mountains yields.

And we will sit upon the rocks,
Seeing the shepherds feed their flocks
By shallow rivers, to whose falls
Melodious birds sing madrigals.

And I will make thee beds of roses,
And a thousand fragrant posies,
A cap of flowers and a kirtle
Embroidered all with leaves of myrtle;

A gown made of the finest wool,
Which from our pretty lambs we pull;
Fair-lined slippers for the cold,
With buckles of the purest gold;

A belt of straw and ivy buds,
With coral clasps and amber studs;
And if these pleasures may thee move,
Come live with me and be my love.
The shepherd swains shall dance and sing
For thy delight each May morning;
If these delights thy mind may move,
Then live with me and be my love.

Christopher Marlowe (1564–93)

I Would Live In Your Love

I would live in your love as the sea-grasses live in the sea,
Borne up by each wave as it passes, drawn down by each
    wave that recedes;

I would empty my soul of the dreams that have
  gathered in me,
I would beat with your heart as it beats,
  I would follow your soul as it leads.

Sara Teasdale (1884–1933)

Perfect Woman

She was a phantom of delight
When first she gleam'd upon my sight;
A lovely apparition, sent
To be a moment's ornament;
Her eyes as stars of twilight fair;
Like twilight's, too, her dusky hair;
But all things else about her drawn
From May-time and the cheerful dawn;
A dancing shape, an image gay,
To haunt, to startle, and waylay.

I saw her upon nearer view,
A Spirit, yet a Woman too!
Her household motions light and free,
And steps of virgin liberty;
A countenance in which did meet
Sweet records, promises as sweet;
A creature not too bright or good
For human nature's daily food;
For transient sorrows, simple wiles,
Praise, blame, love, kisses, tears, and smiles.

And now I see with eye serene
The very pulse of the machine;
A being breathing thoughtful breath,
A traveller between life and death;
The reason firm, the temperate will,
Endurance, foresight, strength, and skill;
A perfect Woman, nobly plann'd,
To warm, to comfort, and command;
And yet a Spirit still, and bright
With something of angelic light.

William Wordsworth (1770–1850)

Love One Another

Love one another, but make not a bond of love
Let it rather be a moving sea between the shores
   of your souls.

Fill each other's cup, but drink not from one cup.
Give one another of your bread, but eat not from
   the same loaf.

Sing and dance together and be joyous,
but let each one of you be alone,
Even as the strings of a lute are alone
though they quiver with the same music.

Give your hearts, but not into each other's keeping;
For only the hand of Life can contain your hearts.

And stand together yet not too near together;
For the pillars of the temple stand apart,
And the oak tree and the cypress grow not in each
   other's shadow.

Khalil Gibran (1883–1931)

Never Marry, but for Love

Never marry but for love;
but see that thou lovest what is lovely.
He that minds a body and not a soul
has not the better part of that relationship,
and will consequently lack
the noblest comfort of a married life.

Between a man and his wife nothing ought rule but love.
As love ought to bring them together, so it is the best way
to keep them well together.

A husband and wife that love one another
show their children that they should do so too.
Others visibly lose their authority in their families by
their contempt of one another, and teach their children to be
unnatural by their own examples.

Let not enjoyment lessen, but augment, affection;
it being the basest of passions to like
when we have not, what we slight when we possess.

Here it is we ought to search out our pleasure,
where the field is large and full of variety,
and of an enduring nature; sickness,
poverty or disgrace being not able to
shake it because it is not under
the moving influences of worldly contingencies.

Nothing can be more entire and without reserve;
nothing more zealous, affectionate and sincere;
nothing more contented than such a couple,
nor greater temporal felicity
than to be one of them.

William Penn (1644–1718)

The Newly-Wedded

Now the rite is duly done,
Now the word is spoken,
And the spell has made us one
Which may ne'er be broken;
Rest we, dearest, in our home,
Roam we o'er the heather:
We shall rest, and we shall roam,
Shall we not together?

From this hour the summer rose
Sweeter breathes to charm us;
From this hour the winter snows
Lighter fall to harm us:

Fair or foul – on land or sea –
Come the wind or weather,
Best and worst, whate'er they be,
We shall share together.

Death, who friend from friend can part,
Brother rend from brother,
Shall but link us, heart and heart,
Closer to each other:
We will call his anger play,
Deem his dart a feather,
When we meet him on our way
Hand in hand together.

Winthrop Mackworth Praed (1802–39)

Two Lovers

Two lovers by a moss-grown spring:
They leaned soft cheeks together there,
Mingled the dark and sunny hair,
And heard the wooing thrushes sing.
O budding time!
O love's blest prime!

Two wedded from the portal stept:
The bells made happy carolings,
The air was soft as fanning wings,
White petals on the pathway slept.
O pure-eyed bride!
O tender pride!

Two faces o'er a cradle bent:
Two hands above the head were locked:
These pressed each other while they rocked,
Those watched a life that love had sent.
O solemn hour!
O hidden power!

Two parents by the evening fire:
The red light fell about their knees
On heads that rose by slow degrees
Like buds upon the lily spire.
O patient life!
O tender strife!

The two still sat together there,
The red light shone about their knees;
But all the heads by slow degrees
Had gone and left that lonely pair.
O voyage fast!
O vanished past!

The red light shone upon the floor
And made the space between them wide;
They drew their chairs up side by side,
Their pale cheeks joined, and said, "Once more!"
O memories!
O past that is!

George Eliot (1819–80)

She Walks in Beauty

She walks in beauty, like the night
Of cloudless climes and starry skies;
And all that's best of dark and bright
Meet in her aspect and her eyes:
Thus mellow'd to that tender light
Which heaven to gaudy day denies.
One shade the more, one ray the less,
Had half impair'd the nameless grace
Which waves in every raven tress,
Or softly lightens o'er her face;
Where thoughts serenely sweet express
How pure, how dear their dwelling-place.

And on that cheek, and o'er that brow,
So soft, so calm, yet eloquent,
The smiles that win, the tints that glow,
But tell of days in goodness spent,
A mind at peace with all below,
A heart whose love is innocent!

George Gordon, Lord Byron (1788–1824)

Love

In peace, Love tunes the shepherd's reed;
In war, he mounts the warrior's steed;
In halls, in gay attire is seen;
In hamlets, dances on the green.
Love rules the court, the camp, the grove,
And men below and saints above;
For love is heaven, and heaven is love.

Sir Walter Scott (1771–1832)

At Last

At last, when all the summer shine
That warmed life's early hours is past,
Your loving fingers seek for mine
And hold them close – at last – at last!
Not oft the robin comes to build
Its nest upon the leafless bough
By autumn robbed, by winter chilled, –
But you, dear heart, you love me now.

Though there are shadows on my brow
And furrows on my cheek, in truth, –
The marks where Time's remorseless plough
Broke up the blooming sward of Youth, –
Though fled is every girlish grace
Might win or hold a lover's vow,
Despite my sad and faded face,
And darkened heart, you love me now!

I count no more my wasted tears;
They left no echo of their fall;
I mourn no more my lonesome years;
This blessed hour atones for all.
I fear not all that Time or Fate
May bring to burden heart or brow, –
Strong in the love that came so late,
Our souls shall keep it always now!

Elizabeth Allen Akers (1832–1911)

Love is Enough

Love is enough: though the World be a-waning,
And the woods have no voice but the voice of complaining,
Though the sky be too dark for dim eyes to discover
The gold-cups and daisies fair blooming thereunder,
Though the hills be held shadows, and the sea a dark wonder,

And this day draw a veil over all deeds pass'd over,
Yet their hands shall not tremble, their feet shall not falter;
The void shall not weary, the fear shall not alter
These lips and these eyes of the loved and the lover.

William Morris (1834–96)

Love

Love is the sunlight of the soul,
That, shining on the silken-tressèd head
Of her we love, around it seems to shed
A golden angel-aureole.

And all her ways seem sweeter ways
Than those of other women in that light:
She has no portion with the pallid night,
But is a part of all fair days.

Joy goes where she goes, and good dreams –
Her smile is tender as an old romance
Of Love that dies not, and her soft eye's glance
Like sunshine set to music seems.

Queen of our fate is she, but crowned
With purple hearts-ease for her womanhood.
There is no place so poor where she has stood
But evermore is holy ground.

An angel from the heaven above
Would not be fair to us as she is fair:
She holds us in a mesh of silken hair,
This one sweet woman whom we love.

We pray thee, Love, our souls to steep
In dreams wherein thy myrtle flowereth;
So when the rose leaves shiver, feeling Death
Pass by, we may remain asleep:

Asleep, with poppies in our hands,
From all the world and all its cares apart –
Cheek close to cheek, heart beating against heart,
While through Life's sandglass run the sands.

Victor James Daley (1858–1905)

My Lady Love

There are none so happy as my love and I,
None so joyous, blithe and free;
The reason is, that I love her,
And the reason is, she loves me.

There are none so sweet as my own fond love,
None so beauteous or true;
Her equal I could never find,
Though I search the whole world thro'.

There's no love so true as my lady sweet;
None so constant to its troth;
There's naught on earth like her so dear,
No queen her equal in her worth.

So there's none so happy as my love and I;
None so blissful, blithe and free,
And the reason is that I am hers,
And she, in truth, belongs to me.

Robert C.O. Benjamin (1855–1900)

Air and Angels

Twice or thrice had I loved thee,
Before I knew thy face or name;
So in a voice, so in a shapeless flame,
Angels affect us oft, and worshipped be;
    Still when, to where thou wert, I came,
Some lovely glorious nothing I did see,
    But since my soul, whose child love is,
Takes limbs of flesh, and else could nothing do,
    More subtle than the parent is
Love must not be, but take a body too,
    And therefore what thou wert, and who
    I bid love ask, and now
That it assume thy body, I allow,
And fix itself in thy lip, eye, and brow

Whilst thus to ballast love, I thought,
And so more steadily to have gone,
With wares which would sink admiration,
I saw, I had love's pinnace overfraught,
    Every thy hair for love to work upon
Is too much, some fitter must be sought;
    For, nor in nothing, nor in things
Extreme, and scatt'ring bright, can love inhere;
    Then as an angel, face and wings
Of air, not pure as it, yet doth wear,
    So thy love may be my love's sphere;
    Just such disparity
As is 'twixt air and angels' purity
'Twixt women's love, and men's will ever be.

John Donne (1572–1631)

Love, Dearest Lady, Such as I Would Speak

Love, dearest Lady, such as I would speak,
Lives not within the humor of the eye; –
Not being but an outward phantasy,
That skims the surface of a tinted cheek, –
Else it would wane with beauty, and grow weak,
As if the rose made summer, – and so lie
Amongst the perishable things that die,
Unlike the love which I would give and seek:
Whose health is of no hue – to feel decay
With cheeks' decay, that have a rosy prime.
Love is its own great loveliness always,
And takes new lustre from the touch of time;
Its bough owns no December and no May,
But bears its blossom into Winter's clime.

Thomas Hood (1799–1845)

The Beloved: Reflections on the Path of the Heart

Tell me, O people, tell me!
Who among you would not wake from
the sleep of life
if love were to brush your spirit with its fingertips?

Who among you would not forsake your
father and your mother
and your home if the girl whom
your heart loved were to call to him?

Who among you would not cross the
seas, traverse deserts,
go over mountains and valleys to reach
the woman whom his spirit has chosen?

What youth would not follow his heart to
the ends of the earth
to breathe the sweetness of his lover's
breath, feel the soft touch of her hands,
delight in the melody of her voice?

What man would not immolate his soul
that its smoke might rise to a god who
would hear his plea
and answer his prayer?

Khalil Gibran (1883–1931)

Happiest

Calling you now, not for your flesh I call,
Nor for the mad, long raptures of the night
And passion in its beauty and its might,
When the ecstatic bodies rise and fall.
I cannot feign: God knows I see it all –
The flaming senses, raving with delight,
The leopards, swift and terrible and white,
Within the loins that shudder as they crawl.

All that could I exultingly forego,
Could I but stand, one flash of time, and see
Your heavenly, entrancing face, and know
I stood most blest of all beneath the sun,
Hearing these words from your fond lips to me:
'I love, love you, and love no other one!'

George Sterling (1869–1926)

My Heart Shall be Thy Garden

My heart shall be thy garden. Come, my own,
Into thy garden; thine be happy hours
Among my fairest thoughts, my tallest flowers,
From root to crowning petal, thine alone.
Thine is the place from where the seeds are sown
Up to the sky inclosed, with all its showers.
But ah, the birds, the birds! Who shall build bowers
To keep these thine? O friend, the birds have flown.

For as these come and go, and quit our pine
To follow the sweet season, or, new-corners,
Sing one song only from our alder-trees,
My heart has thoughts, which, though thine eyes hold mine,
Flit to the silent world and other summers,
With wings that dip beyond the silver seas.

Alice Meynell (1847–1922)

Beautiful Dreamer

Beautiful dreamer, wake unto me,
Starlight and dewdrops are waiting for thee;
Sounds of the rude world heard in the day,
Lull'd by the moonlight have all pass'd away!

Beautiful dreamer, queen of my song,
List while I woo thee with soft melody;
Gone are the cares of life's busy throng,
Beautiful dreamer, awake unto me!

Beautiful dreamer, out on the sea
Mermaids are chaunting the wild lorelei;
Over the streamlet vapors are borne,
Waiting to fade at the bright coming morn.

Beautiful dreamer, beam on my heart,
E'en as the morn on the streamlet and sea;
Then will all clouds of sorrow depart,
Beautiful dreamer, awake unto me!

Stephen Foster (1826–64)

Somewhere

Somewhere there waiteth in this world of ours
for one lone soul, another lonely soul –
Each chasing each through all the weary hours,
And meeting strangely at one sudden goal;

Then blend they – like green leaves with golden flowers,
Into one beautiful and perfect whole –
And life's long night is ended, and the way
Lies open onward to eternal day.

Sir Edwin Arnold (1832–1904)

Sonnet XIV

If thou must love me, let it be for nought
Except for love's sake only. Do not say
'I love her for her smile – her look – her way
Of speaking gently, – for a trick of thought
That falls in well with mine, and certes brought
A sense of pleasant ease on such a day' –
For these things in themselves, Beloved, may
Be changed, or change for thee, – and love, so wrought,
May be unwrought so. Neither love me for
Thine own dear pity's wiping my cheeks dry, –
A creature might forget to weep, who bore
Thy comfort long, and lose thy love thereby!
But love me for love's sake, that evermore
Thou may'st love on, through love's eternity.

Elizabeth Barrett Browning (1806–61)

A Dream

I dreamed that I loved a sweet maiden,
With hair of bright rippling gold;
And the story I told of my love to her
Is the same one that's ever been told.

I dreamed that her eyes, bright and gladsome,
Were dark as the raven's black wing;
And I thought that upon her third finger
I placed a plain gold wedding ring.

I dreamed that her lips, red as cherries,
Were dangerously close to my own;
And the kiss that I gave her whilst dreaming,
Awoke me, so loud was its tone.

But when I awoke I remembered
The cause of my fancy's sweet flight,
And the reason of happy dreaming,
Which made blissful the visions of night.

'Twas a picture which looked from the canvas,
Painted though perfect to life,
And so sweet was the face and the tresses,
I dreamed that I made her my wife.

Robert C.O. Benjamin (1855–1900)

True Woman – Her Love

She loves him; for her infinite soul is Love,
And he her lodestar. Passion in her is
A glass facing his fire, where the bright bliss
Is mirrored, and the heat returned. Yet move
That glass, a stranger's amorous flame to prove,
And it shall turn, by instant contraries,
Ice to the moon; while her pure fire to his
For whom it burns, clings close i' the heart's alcove.

Lo! they are one. With wifely breast to breast
And circling arms, she welcomes all command
Of love, – her soul to answering ardours fann'd:
Yet as morn springs or twilight sinks to rest,
Ah! who shall say she deems not loveliest
The hour of sisterly sweet hand-in-hand?

Dante Gabriel Rossetti (1828–82)

A White Rose

The red rose whispers of passion,
And the white rose breathes of love;
O the red rose is a falcon,
And the white rose is a dove.

But I send you a cream-white rosebud
With a flush on its petal tips;
For the love that is purest and sweetest
Has a kiss of desire on the lips.

John Boyle O'Reilly (1844–90)

HOLIDAYS:
VALENTINE'S DAY

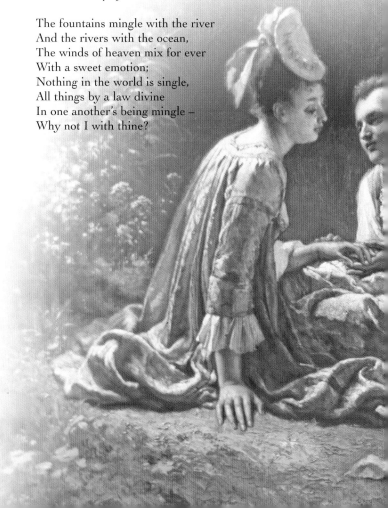

Love's Philosophy

The fountains mingle with the river
And the rivers with the ocean,
The winds of heaven mix for ever
With a sweet emotion;
Nothing in the world is single,
All things by a law divine
In one another's being mingle –
Why not I with thine?

See the mountains kiss high heaven,
And the waves clasp one another;
No sister-flower would be forgiven
If it disdain'd its brother;
And the sunlight clasps the earth,
And the moonbeams kiss the sea –
What is all this sweet work worth
If thou kiss not me?

Percy Bysshe Shelley (1792–1822)

But Were I Loved

BUT were I loved, as I desire to be,
What is there in the great sphere of the earth,
And range of evil between death and birth,
That I should fear, – if I were loved by thee?
All the inner, all the outer world of pain
Clear Love would pierce and cleave, if thou wert mine,
As I have heard that, somewhere in the main,
Fresh-water springs come up through bitter brine.
'Twere joy, not fear, clasped hand-in-hand with thee,
To wait for death – mute – careless of all ills,
Apart upon a mountain, tho' the surge
Of some new deluge from a thousand hills
Flung leagues of roaring foam into the gorge
Below us, as far on as eye could see.

Alfred, Lord Tennyson (1809–92)

Time of Roses

It was not in the Winter
Our loving lot was cast;
It was the time of roses –
We pluck'd them as we pass'd!

That churlish season never frown'd
On early lovers yet:
O no – the world was newly crown'd
With flowers when first we met!

'Twas twilight, and I bade you go,
But still you held me fast;
It was the time of roses –
We pluck'd them as we pass'd!

Thomas Hood (1799–1845)

A Red, Red Rose

Tune: *Major Graham*

O my luve's like a red, red rose
That's newly sprung in June;
O my luve's like the melodie
That's sweetly play'd in tune.

As fair thou art, my bonnie lass,
So deep in luve am I,
And I will luve thee still, my Dear,
Till a' the seas gang dry.

Till a' the seas gang dry, my Dear,
And the rocks melt wi' the sun:
I will luve thee still, my Dear,
While the sands o' life shall run.

And fare thee weel, my only Luve,
And fare thee weel a while!
And I will come again, my Luve,
Tho' it were ten thousand mile!

Robert Burns (1759–96)

Out Upon it, I Have Loved

Out upon it, I have loved
Three whole days together;
And am like to love three more,
If it prove fair weather.

Time shall moult away his wings
Ere he shall discover
In the whole wide world again
Such a constant lover.

But the spite on't is, no praise
Is due at all to me:
Love with me had made no stays
Had it any been but she.

Had it any been but she,
And that very face,
There had been at least ere this
A dozen dozen in her place.

Sir John Suckling (1609–42)

I Love Thee

I love thee – I love thee!
'Tis all that I can say; –
It is my vision in the night,
My dreaming in the day;
The very echo of my heart,
The blessing when I pray:
I love thee – I love thee!
Is all that I can say.
I love thee – I love thee!
Is ever on my tongue;
In all my proudest poesy
That chorus still is sung;
It is the verdict of my eyes,
Amidst the gay and young:
I love thee – I love thee!
A thousand maids among.
I love thee – I love thee!
Thy bright hazel glance,
The mellow lute upon those lips,
Whose tender tones entrance;
But most, dear heart of hearts, thy proofs
That still these words enhance,
I love thee – I love thee!
Whatever be thy chance.

Thomas Hood (1799–1845)

The Secret

I loved thee, though I told thee not,
Right earlily and long,
Thou wert my joy in every spot,
My theme in every song.

And when I saw a stranger face
Where beauty held the claim,
I gave it like a secret grace
The being of thy name.

And all the charms of face or voice
Which I in others see
Are but the recollected choice
Of what I felt for thee.

John Clare (1793–1864)

Who Ever Loved, That Loved Not at First Sight?

It lies not in our power to love or hate,
For will in us is overruled by fate.
When two are stripped, long ere the course begin,
We wish that one should love, the other win;
And one especially do we affect
Of two gold ingots, like in each respect:
The reason no man knows; let it suffice
What we behold is censured by our eyes.
Where both deliberate, the love is slight:
Who ever loved, that loved not at first sight?

Christopher Marlowe (1564–93)

O Mistress Mine

O Mistress mine, where are you roaming?
O stay and hear! your true-love's coming
That can sing both high and low;
Trip no further, pretty sweeting,
Journeys end in lovers' meeting –
Every wise man's son doth know.

What is love? 'tis not hereafter;
Present mirth hath present laughter;
What's to come is still unsure:
In delay there lies no plenty, –
Then come kiss me, Sweet-and-twenty,
Youth's a stuff will not endure.

William Shakespeare (1564–1616)

Wooing Song

Love is the blossom where there blows
Every thing that lives or grows:
Love doth make the Heav'ns to move,
And the Sun doth burn in love:
Love the strong and weak doth yoke,
And makes the ivy climb the oak,
Under whose shadows lions wild,
Soften'd by love, grow tame and mild:
Love no med'cine can appease,
He burns the fishes in the seas:
Not all the skill his wounds can stench,
Not all the sea his fire can quench.
Love did make the bloody spear
Once a leavy coat to wear,
While in his leaves there shrouded lay
Sweet birds, for love that sing and play
And of all love's joyful flame
I the bud and blossom am.
Only bend thy knee to me,
Thy wooing shall thy winning be!

See, see the flowers that below
Now as fresh as morning blow;
And of all the virgin rose
That as bright Aurora shows;
How they all unleavèd die,
Losing their virginity!
Like unto a summer shade,
But now born, and now they fade.

Every thing doth pass away;
There is danger in delay:
Come, come, gather then the rose,
Gather it, or it you lose!
All the sand of Tagus' shore
Into my bosom casts his ore:
All the valleys' swimming corn
To my house is yearly borne:
Every grape of every vine
Is gladly bruised to make me wine:
While ten thousand kings, as proud,
To carry up my train have bow'd,
And a world of ladies send me
In my chambers to attend me:
All the stars in Heav'n that shine,
And ten thousand more, are mine:
Only bend thy knee to me,
Thy wooing shall thy winning be!

Giles Fletcher (1586–1623)

Sonnet 18

Shall I compare thee to a summer's day?
Thou art more lovely and more temperate:
Rough winds do shake the darling buds of May,
And summer's lease hath all too short a date:
Sometime too hot the eye of heaven shines,
And often is his gold complexion dimm'd;
And every fair from fair sometime declines,
By chance, or nature's changing course untrimm'd;
But thy eternal summer shall not fade,
Nor lose possession of that fair thou ow'st,
Nor shall death brag thou wander'st in his shade,
When in eternal lines to time thou grow'st;
So long as men can breathe, or eyes can see,
So long lives this, and this gives life to thee.

William Shakespeare (1564–1616)

Flame

Thou art that madness of supreme desire,
Which lacking, beauty is but dross and clay.
Within thy veins is all the fire of day
And all the stars divinity of fire.
Thine are the lips and loins that never tire,
And thine the bliss that makes my soul dismay.
Upon thy breast what god at midnight lay,
To make thy flesh the music of his lyre?
Ah! such alone should know thy loveliness!
Ah! such alone should know thy full caress,
O goddess of intolerable delight!
I beg of Fate the guerdon and the grace,
Far beyond death, to know in thine embrace
Eternal rapture in eternal night.

George Sterling (1869–1926)

Sonnet II

As strong, as deep, as wide as is the sea,
Though by the wind made restless as the wind,
By billows fretted and by rocks confined,
So strong, so deep, so wide my love for thee.
And as the sea; though oft huge waves arise,
So oft that calms can never quite assuage,
So huge that ocean's whole self seems to rage;
Yet tranquil, deep, beneath the tempest lies:
So my great love for thee lies tranquil, deep,
Forever; though above it passions fierce,
Ambition, hatred, jealousy; like waves
That seem from earth's core to the sky to leap,
But ocean's depths can never really pierce;
Hide its great calm, while all the surface raves.

Francis William Bourdillon (1852–1921)

A Valentine to My Wife

Accept, dear girl, this little token,
And if between the lines you seek,
You'll find the love I've often spoken –
The love my dying lips shall speak.

Our little ones are making merry
O'er am'rous ditties rhymed in jest,
But in these words (though awkward – very)
The genuine article's expressed.

You are as fair and sweet and tender,
Dear brown-eyed little sweetheart mine,
As when, a callow youth and slender,
I asked to be your Valentine.

What though these years of ours be fleeting?
What though the years of youth be flown?
I'll mock old Tempus with repeating,
'I love my love and her alone!'

And when I fall before his reaping,
And when my stuttering speech is dumb,
Think not my love is dead or sleeping,
But that it waits for you to come.

So take, dear love, this little token,
And if there speaks in any line
The sentiment I'd fain have spoken,
Say, will you kiss your Valentine?

Eugene Field (1850–95)

HOLIDAYS:
MOTHER'S DAY

Only One

Hundreds of stars in the pretty sky,
Hundreds of shells on the shore together,
Hundreds of birds that go singing by,
Hundreds of birds in the sunny weather.

Hundreds of dewdrops to greet the dawn,
Hundreds of bees in the purple clover,
Hundreds of butterflies on the lawn,
But only one mother the wide world over.

George Cooper (1840–1927)

To My Mother

They tell us of an Indian tree
    Which howsoe'er the sun and sky
May tempt its boughs to wander free,
    And shoot and blossom, wide and high,
Far better loves to bend its arms
    Downward again to that dear earth
From which the life that fills and warms
    Its grateful being, first had birth,
'Tis thus, though wooed by flattering friends,
    And fed with fame (if fame it may be),
This heart, my own dear mother, bends,
    With love's true instinct, back to thee!

Thomas Moore (1779–1852)

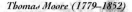

My Blessed Mother

My blessed Mother dozing in her chair
On Christmas Day seem'd an embodied Love,
A comfortable Love with soft brown hair
Softened and silvered to a tint of dove;
A better sort of Venus with an air
Angelical from thoughts that dwell above;
A wiser Pallas in whose body fair
Enshrined a blessed soul looks out thereof.
Winter brought holly then;
Now spring has brought
Paler and frailer snowdrops shivering;
And I have brought a simple humble thought –
I her devoted duteous Valentine –
A lifelong thought which thrills this song I sing,
A lifelong love to this dear Saint of mine.

Christina Georgina Rossetti (1830–94)

My Vision

Wherever my feet may wander
    Wherever I chance to be,
There comes, with the coming of even' time
    A vision sweet to me.
I see my mother sitting
    In the old familiar place,
And she rocks to the tune her needles sing,
    And thinks of an absent face.

I can hear the roar of the city
    About me now as I write;
But over a hundred miles of snow
    My thought-steeds fly tonight,
To the dear little cozy cottage,
    And the room where mother sits,
And slowly rocks in her easy chair
    And thinks of me as she knits.

Sometimes with the merry dancers
    When my feet are keeping time,
And my heart beats high, as young hearts will,
    To the music's rhythmic chime.
My spirit slips over the distance
    Over the glitter and whirl,
To my mother who sits, and rocks, and knits,
    And thinks of her 'little girl.'

And when I listen to voices that flatter,
    And smile, as women do,
To whispered words that may be sweet,
    But are not always true;
I think of the sweet, quaint picture
    Afar in quiet ways,
And I know one smile of my mother's eyes
    Is better than all their praise.

And I know I can never wander
    Far from the path of right,
Though snares are set for a woman's feet
    In places that seem most bright.
For the vision is with me always,
    Wherever I chance to be,
Of mother sitting, rocking, and knitting,
    Thinking and praying for me.

Ella Wheeler Wilcox (1850–1919)

Songs For My Mother

Her Hands

My mother's hands are cool and fair,
They can do anything.
Delicate mercies hide them there
Like flowers in the spring.

When I was small and could not sleep,
She used to come to me,
And with my cheek upon her hand
How sure my rest would be.

For everything she ever touched
Of beautiful or fine,
Their memories living in her hands
Would warm that sleep of mine.

Her hands remember how they played
One time in meadow streams, –
And all the flickering song and shade
Of water took my dreams.

Swift through her haunted fingers pass
Memories of garden things; –
I dipped my face in flowers and grass
And sounds of hidden wings.

One time she touched the cloud that kissed
Brown pastures bleak and far; –
I leaned my cheek into a mist
And thought I was a star.

All this was very long ago
And I am grown; but yet
The hand that lured my slumber so
I never can forget.

For still when drowsiness comes on
It seems so soft and cool,
Shaped happily beneath my cheek,
Hollow and beautiful.

Her Words

My mother has the prettiest tricks
Of words and words and words.
Her talk comes out as smooth and sleek
As breasts of singing birds.

She shapes her speech all silver fine
Because she loves it so.
And her own eyes begin to shine
To hear her stories grow.

And if she goes to make a call
Or out to take a walk
We leave our work when she returns
And run to hear her talk.

We had not dreamed these things were so
Of sorrow and of mirth.
Her speech is as a thousand eyes
Through which we see the earth.

God wove a web of loveliness,
Of clouds and stars and birds,
But made not anything at all
So beautiful as words.

They shine around our simple earth
With golden shadowings,
And every common thing they touch
Is exquisite with wings.

There's nothing poor and nothing small
But is made fair with them.
They are the hands of living faith
That touch the garment's hem.

They are as fair as bloom or air,
They shine like any star,
And I am rich who learned from her
How beautiful they are.

Anna Hempstead Branch (1875–1937)

My Mother

God made my mother on an April day,
From sorrow and the mist along the sea,
Lost birds' and wanderers' songs and ocean spray,
And the moon loved her wandering jealously.

Beside the ocean's din she combed her hair,
Singing the nocturne of the passing ships,
Before her earthly lover found her there
And kissed away the music from her lips.

She came unto the hills and saw the change
That brings the swallow and the geese in turns.
But there was not a grief she deemèd strange,
For there is that in her which always mourns.

Kind heart she has for all on hill or wave
Whose hopes grew wings like ants to fly away.
I bless the God Who such a mother gave
This poor bird-hearted singer of a day.

Francis Ledwidge (1887–1917)

Family Love

I adore my dear mother,
I adore my dear father too;
No one loves me as much
As they know how to love me.

When I sleep, they keep watch over me;
When I cry they are sad with me;
When I laugh they smile with me:
My laugh is the sunshine for them.

They tenderly teach me
To be happy and nice.
My father does his best for me;
My mother prays always for me.

I adore my dear mother,
I adore my dear father too.
No one loves me as much
As they know how to love me.

Amado Ruiz de Nervo (1870–1919)

HOLIDAYS:
EASTER

Good Friday in My Heart

GOOD FRIDAY in my heart! Fear and affright!
My thoughts are the Disciples when they fled,
My words the words that priest and soldier said,
My deed the spear to desecrate the dead.
And day, Thy death therein, is changed to night.

Then Easter in my heart sends up the sun.
My thoughts are Mary, when she turned to see.
My words are Peter, answering, 'Lov'st thou Me?'
My deeds are all Thine own drawn close to Thee,
And night and day, since Thou dost rise, are one.

Mary Elizabeth Coleridge (1861–1907)

Easter

Rise heart; thy Lord is risen. Sing His praise
 Without delayes,
Who takes thee by the hand, that thou likewise
 With Him mayst rise:
That, as His death calcinèd thee to dust,
His life may make thee gold, and much more just.

Awake, my lute, and struggle for thy part
 With all thy art,
The crosse taught all wood to resound His name
 Who bore the same.
His stretchèd sinews taught all strings, what key
Is best to celebrate this most high day.

Consort, both heart and lute, and twist a song
 Pleasant and long;
Or since all musick is but three parts vied,
 And multiplied;
O let thy blessèd Spirit bear a part,
And make up our defects with His sweet art.

 I got me flowers to straw thy way;
I got me boughs off many a tree:
 But thou wast up by break of day,
And brought'st thy sweets along with thee.

The Sunne arising in the East,
Though He give light, and th' East perfume;
    If they should offer to contest
With Thy arising, they presume.

    Can there be any day but this,
Though many sunnes to shine endeavour?
    We count three hundred, but we misse:
There is but one, and that one ever.

George Herbert (1593–1633)

Easter Week

See the land, her Easter keeping,
Rises as her Maker rose.
Seeds, so long in darkness sleeping,
Burst at last from winter snows.
Earth with heaven above rejoices;
Fields and gardens hail the spring;
Shaws and woodlands ring with voices,
While the wild birds build and sing.

You, to whom your Maker granted
Powers to those sweet birds unknown,
Use the craft by God implanted;
Use the reason not your own.
Here, while heaven and earth rejoices,
Each his Easter tribute bring –
Work of fingers, chant of voices,
Like the birds who build and sing.

Charles Kingsley (1819–75)

Easter

The air is like a butterfly
With frail blue wings.
The happy earth looks at the sky
And sings.

Alfred Joyce Kilmer (1886–1918)

Easter

MOST glorious Lord of Lyfe! that, on this day,
Didst make Thy triumph over death and sin;
And, having harrow'd hell, didst bring away
Captivity thence captive, us to win:
This joyous day, deare Lord, with joy begin;
And grant that we, for whom thou diddest dye,
Being with Thy deare blood clene washt from sin,
May live for ever in felicity!

And that Thy love we weighing worthily,
May likewise love Thee for the same againe;
And for Thy sake, that all lyke deare didst buy,
With love may one another entertayne!
   So let us love, deare Love, lyke as we ought,
   Love is the lesson which the Lord us taught.

Edmund Spenser (1552–99)

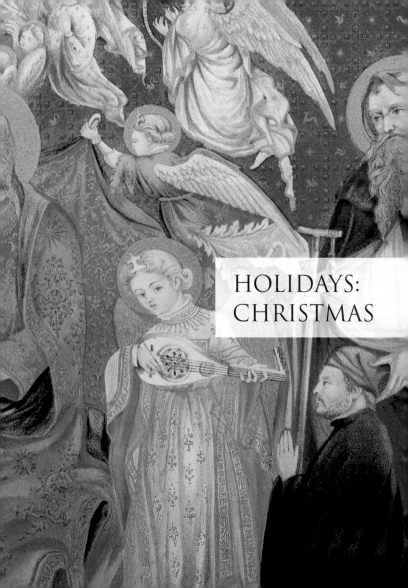

HOLIDAYS:
CHRISTMAS

Christmas Everywhere

Everywhere, everywhere, Christmas tonight!
Christmas in lands of the fir-tree and pine,
Christmas in lands of the palm-tree and vine,
Christmas where snow peaks stand solemn and white,
Christmas where cornfields stand sunny and bright.
Christmas where children are hopeful and gay,
Christmas where old men are patient and gray,
Christmas where peace, like a dove in his flight,
Broods o'er brave men in the thick of the fight;
Everywhere, everywhere, Christmas tonight!
For the Christ-child who comes is the Master of all;
No palace too great, no cottage too small.

Phillips Brooks (1835–93)

From Our Happy Home

From our happy home
Through the world we roam
One week in all the year,
Making winter spring
With the joy we bring
For Christmas-tide is here.

Now the eastern star
Shines from afar
To light the poorest home;
Hearts warmer grow,
Gifts freely flow,
For Christmas-tide has come.

Now gay trees rise
Before young eyes,
Abloom with tempting cheer;
Blithe voices sing,
And blithe bells ring,
For Christmas-tide is here.

Oh, happy chime,
Oh, blessed time,
That draws us all so near!
'Welcome, dear day,'
All creatures say,
For Christmas-tide is here.

Louisa May Alcott (1832–88)

Ceremonies for Christmas

Come, bring with a noise,
My merry, merry boys,
The Christmas Log to the firing;
While my good Dame, she
Bids ye all be free;
And drink to your heart's desiring.

With the last year's brand
Light the new block, and
For good success in his spending,
On your Psaltries play,
That sweet luck may
Come while the log is a-tinding.

Drink now the strong beer,
Cut the white loaf here,
The while the meat is a-shredding;
For the rare mince-pie
And the plums stand by
To fill the paste that's a-kneading.

Robert Herrick (1591–1674)

The Night Before Christmas

Twas the night before Christmas, when all through the house
Not a creature was stirring, not even a mouse.
The stockings were hung by the chimney with care,
In hopes that St Nicholas soon would be there.

The children were nestled all snug in their beds,
While visions of sugar-plums danced in their heads.
And mamma in her 'kerchief, and I in my cap,
Had just settled our brains for a long winter's nap.

When out on the lawn there arose such a clatter,
I sprang from the bed to see what was the matter.
Away to the window I flew like a flash,
Tore open the shutters and threw up the sash.

The moon on the breast of the new-fallen snow
Gave the lustre of mid-day to objects below.
When, what to my wondering eyes should appear,
But a miniature sleigh, and eight tiny reindeer.

With a little old driver, so lively and quick,
I knew in a moment it must be St Nick.
More rapid than eagles his coursers they came,
And he whistled, and shouted, and called them by name!

'Now Dasher! now, Dancer! now, Prancer and Vixen!
On, Comet! On, Cupid! on, Donner and Blitzen!
To the top of the porch! to the top of the wall!
Now dash away! Dash away! Dash away all!'

As dry leaves that before the wild hurricane fly,
When they meet with an obstacle, mount to the sky
So up to the house-top the coursers they flew
With the sleigh full of Toys, and St Nicholas too.

And then, in a twinkling, I heard on the roo
The prancing and pawing of each little hoof.
As I drew in my head, and was turning around
Down the chimney St Nicholas came with a bound.

He was dressed all in fur, from his head to his foot,
And his clothes were all tarnished with ashes and soot.
A bundle of Toys he had flung on his back,
And he looked like a peddler, just opening his pack.

His eyes – how they twinkled! his dimples how merry!
His cheeks were like roses, his nose like a cherry!
His droll little mouth was drawn up like a bow,
And the beard of his chin was as white as the snow.

The stump of a pipe he held tight in his teeth,
And the smoke it encircled his head like a wreath.
He had a broad face and a little round belly,
That shook when he laughed, like a bowlful of jelly!

He was chubby and plump, a right jolly old elf,
And I laughed when I saw him, in spite of myself!
A wink of his eye and a twist of his head,
Soon gave me to know I had nothing to dread.

He spoke not a word, but went straight to his work,
And filled all the stockings, then turned with a jerk.
And laying his finger aside of his nose,
And giving a nod, up the chimney he rose!

He sprang to his sleigh, to his team gave a whistle,
And away they all flew like the down of a thistle.
But I heard him exclaim, 'ere he drove out of sight,
'Happy Christmas to all, and to all a good-night!'

Clement Clarke Moore (1779–1863)

An Extract from A Christmas Carol

So now is come our joyful'st feast,
Let every man be jolly.
Each room with ivy leaves is drest,
And every post with holly.
Though some churls at our mirth repine,
Round your foreheads garlands twine,
Drown sorrow in a cup of wine,
And let us all be merry.

Now all our neighbours' chimneys smoke,
And Christmas blocks are burning;
Their ovens they with bak'd-meats choke,
And all their spits are turning.
Without the door let sorrow lie,
And if for cold it hap to die,
We'll bury 't in a Christmas pie,
And evermore be merry.

Now every lad is wondrous trim,
And no man minds his labour;
Our lasses have provided them
A bag-pipe and a tabor.
Young men and maids and girls and boys
Give life to one another's joys,
And you anon shall by their noise
Perceive that they are merry.

Rank misers now do sparing shun,
Their hall of music soundeth,
And dogs thence with whole shoulders run,
So all things there aboundeth.
The country folk themselves advance,
For crowdy-mutton's come out of France.
And Jack shall pipe and Jill shall dance,
And all the town be merry.

Ned Swash hath fetch'd his bands from pawn,
And all his best apparel;
Brisk Nell hath bought a ruff of lawn
With droppings of the barrel;
And those that hardly all the year
Had bread to eat or rags to wear,
Will have both clothes and dainty fare,
And all the day be merry.

Now poor men to the justices
With capons make their arrants,
And if they hap to fail of these
They plague them with their warrants.
But now they feed them with good cheer,
And what they want they take in beer,
For Christmas comes but once a year,
And then they shall be merry.

Then wherefore in these merry days
Should we, I pray, be duller?
No, let us sing some roundelays
To make our mirth the fuller.
And, whilst thus inspir'd we sing,
Let all the streets with echoes ring,
Woods and hills and everything,
Bear witness we are merry.

George Withers (1588–1667)

For Christmas Day

Hark, how all the welkin rings,
'Glory to the King of kings;
Peace on earth, and mercy mild,
God and sinners reconcil'd!'

Joyful, all ye nations, rise,
Join the triumph of the skies;
Universal nature say,
'Christ the Lord is born to-day!'

Christ, by highest Heaven ador'd,
Christ, the everlasting Lord:
Late in time behold him come,
Offspring of a virgin's womb!

Veil'd in flesh, the Godhead see,
Hail th' incarnate Deity!
Pleas'd as man with men to appear,
Jesus, our Immanuel here!

Hail, the heavenly Prince of Peace,
Hail, the Sun of Righteousness!
Light and life to all he brings,
Risen with healing in his wings.

Mild he lays his glory by,
Born that man no more may die;
Born to raise the sons of earth;
Born to give them second birth.

Come, desire of nations, come,
Fix in us thy humble home;
Rise, the woman's conquering seed,
Bruise in us the serpent's head.

Now display thy saving power,
Ruin'd nature now restore;
Now in mystic union join
Thine to ours, and ours to thine.

Adam's likeness, Lord, efface,
Stamp thy image in its place.
Second Adam from above,
Reinstate us in thy love.

Let us thee, though lost, regain,
Thee, the life, the inner man:
O, to all thyself impart,
Form'd in each believing heart.

Charles Wesley (1707–88)

FUNERALS

Eulogy for a Veteran

Do not stand at my grave and weep
I am not there, I do not sleep.

I am a thousand winds that blow
I am the diamond glint of snow

I am the sunlight on ripened grain
I am the gentle autumn rain

When you awaken in the morning's hush
I am the swift uplifting rush
of quiet birds in circled flight
I am the soft stars that shine at night

Do not stand at my grave and cry,
I am not there, I did not die.

Author Unknown

'In Memoriam' A.H.H.

STRONG Son of God, immortal Love,
   Whom we, that have not seen thy face,
   By faith, and faith alone, embrace,
Believing where we cannot prove;

Thine are these orbs of light and shade;
   Thou madest Life in man and brute;
   Thou madest Death; and lo, thy foot
Is on the skull which thou hast made.

Thou wilt not leave us in the dust:
    Thou madest man, he knows not why,
    He thinks he was not made to die;
And thou hast made him: thou art just.

Thou seemest human and divine,
    The highest, holiest manhood, thou:
    Our wills are ours, we know not how;
Our wills are ours, to make them thine.

Our little systems have their day;
    They have their day and cease to be:
    They are but broken lights of thee,
And thou, O Lord, art more than they.

We have but faith: we cannot know;
    For knowledge is of things we see;
    And yet we trust it comes from thee,
A beam in darkness: let it grow.

Let knowledge grow from more to more,
    But more of reverence in us dwell;
    That mind and soul, according well,
May make one music as before,

But vaster. We are fools and slight;
　　We mock thee when we do not fear:
　　But help thy foolish ones to bear;
Help thy vain worlds to bear thy light.

Forgive what seem'd my sin in me;
　　What seem'd my worth since I began;
　　For merit lives from man to man,
And not from man, O Lord, to thee.

Forgive my grief for one removed,
　　Thy creature, whom I found so fair.
　　I trust he lives in thee, and there
I find him worthier to be loved.

Forgive these wild and wandering cries,
　　Confusions of a wasted youth;
　　Forgive them where they fail in truth,
And in thy wisdom make me wise.

Alfred, Lord Tennyson (1809–92)

Parting

There's no use in weeping,
Though we are condemned to part:
There's such a thing as keeping
A remembrance in one's heart:

There's such a thing as dwelling
On the thought ourselves have nurs'd,
And with scorn and courage telling
The world to do its worst.

We'll not let its follies grieve us,
We'll just take them as they come;
And then every day will leave us
A merry laugh for home.

When we've left each friend and brother,
When we're parted wide and far,
We will think of one another,
As even better than we are.

Every glorious sight above us,
Every pleasant sight beneath,
We'll connect with those that love us,
Whom we truly love till death!

In the evening, when we're sitting
By the fire perchance alone,
Then shall heart with warm heart meeting,
Give responsive tone for tone.

We can burst the bonds which chain us,
Which cold human hands have wrought,
And where none shall dare restrain us
We can meet again, in thought.

So there's no use in weeping,
Bear a cheerful spirit still;
Never doubt that Fate is keeping
Future good for present ill!

Charlotte Brontë (1816–55)

Tomorrow at Dawn

Tomorrow, at dawn, at the hour when the countryside whitens,
I will set out. You see, I know that you wait for me.
I will go by the forest, I will go by the mountain.
I can no longer remain far from you.

I will walk with my eyes fixed on my thoughts,
Seeing nothing of outdoors, hearing no noise
Alone, unknown, my back curved, my hands crossed,
Sorrowed, and the day for me will be as the night.

I will not look at the gold of evening which falls,
Nor the distant sails going down towards Harfleur,
And when I arrive, I will place on your tomb
A bouquet of green holly and of flowering heather.

Victor Hugo (1802–85)

The Meeting

We started speaking,
Looked at each other, then turned away.
The tears kept rising to my eyes.
But I could not weep.
I wanted to take your hand
But my hand trembled.
You kept counting the days
Before we should meet again.
But both of us felt in our hearts
That we parted for ever and ever.
The ticking of the little clock filled the quiet room.
'Listen,' I said. 'It is so loud,
Like a horse galloping on a lonely road,
As loud as a horse galloping past in the night.'
You shut me up in your arms.
But the sound of the clock stifled our hearts' beating.
You said, 'I cannot go: all that is living of me
Is here for ever and ever.'
Then you went.
The world changed. The sound of the clock grew fainter,
Dwindled away, became a minute thing.
I whispered in the darkness. 'If it stops, I shall die.'

Katherine Mansfield (1888–1923)

A Golden Day

I found you and I lost you,
All on a gleaming day.
The day was filled with sunshine,
And the land was full of May.
A golden bird was singing
Its melody divine,
I found you and I loved you,
And all the world was mine.
I found you and I lost you,
All on a golden day,
But when I dream of you, dear,
It is always brimming May.

Paul Laurence Dunbar (1872–1906)

Missing

You walked beside me, quick and free;
With lingering touch you grasped my hand;
Your eyes looked laughingly in mine;
And now – I cannot understand.

I long for you, I mourn for you,
Through all the dark and lonely hours.
Heavy the weight the pallmen lift,
And cover silently with flowers.

Sarah Orne Jewett (1849–1909)

You and I

My hand is lonely for your clasping, dear;
My ear is tired waiting for your call.
I want your strength to help, your laugh to cheer;
Heart, soul and senses need you, one and all.
I droop without your full, frank sympathy;
We ought to be together, you and I;
We want each other so, to comprehend
The dream, the hope, things planned, or seen, or wrought.
Companion, comforter and guide and friend,
As much as love asks love, does thought ask thought.
Life is so short, so fast the lone hours fly,
We ought to be together, you and I.

Henry Alford (1810–71)

A Reminiscence

Yes, thou art gone! And never more
Thy sunny smile shall gladden me;
But I may pass the old church door,
And pace the floor that covers thee,

May stand upon the cold, damp stone,
And think that, frozen, lies below
The lightest heart that I have known,
The kindest I shall ever know.

Yet, though I cannot see thee more,
'Tis still a comfort to have seen;
And though thy transient life is o'er,
'Tis sweet to think that thou hast been;

To think a soul so near divine,
Within a form, so angel fair,
United to a heart like thine,
Has gladdened once our humble sphere.

Anne Brontë (1820–49)

Do I Love Thee?

I ask my heart, 'Do I love thee?'
But how can I e'er forget
The feelings of joy and rapture
That thrilled me when first we met?
The memory of each glad meeting
Is treasured within my heart,
Which has well-nigh ceased its beating,
Since, in sorrow, we had to part.

Each night, as I seek my pillow,
I murmur a prayer for thee,
I breathe thy name, as the sunbeams
Flash red on the eastern sea.
Thy spirit is still the beacon
That guides me 'mid care and strife,
And there 'twill remain for ever,
My darling, my love, my life.

Thomas Edward Spencer (1845–1911)

Remember

Remember me when I am gone away,
    Gone far away into the silent land;
    When you can no more hold me by the hand,
Nor I half turn to go yet turning stay.
Remember me when no more day by day
    You tell me of our future that you plann'd:
    Only remember me; you understand
It will be late to counsel then or pray.
Yet if you should forget me for a while
    And afterwards remember, do not grieve:
    For if the darkness and corruption leave
    A vestige of the thoughts that once I had,
Better by far you should forget and smile
    Than that you should remember and be sad.

Christina Georgina Rossetti (1830–94)

Grief

O who will give me tears? Come, all ye springs,
Dwell in my head and eyes: come, clouds and rain:
My grief hath need of all the wat'ry things,
That nature hath produc'd. Let ev'ry vein
Suck up a river to supply mine eyes,
My weary weeping eyes, too drie for me,
Unlesse they get new conduits, new supplies,
To bear them out, and with my state agree.
What are two shallow foords, two little spouts
Of a lesse world? the greater is but small,
A narrow cupboard for my griefs and doubts,
Which want provision in the midst of all.
Verses, ye are too fine a thing, too wise
For my rough sorrows: cease, be dumb and mute,
Give up your feet and running to mine eyes,
And keep your measures for some lover's lute,
Whose grief allows him musick and a ryme:
For mine excludes both measure, tune, and time.
    Alas, my God!

George Herbert (1593–1633)

Extract from A Baby's Death

A little soul scarce fledged for earth
Takes wing with heaven again for goal
Even while we hailed as fresh from birth
    A little soul.

Our thoughts ring sad as bells that toll,
Not knowing beyond this blind world's girth
What things are writ in heaven's full scroll.

Our fruitfulness is there but dearth,
And all things held in time's control
Seem there, perchance, ill dreams, not worth
    A little soul.

The little feet that never trod
Earth, never strayed in field or street,
What hand leads upward back to God
    The little feet?

A rose in June's most honied heat,
When life makes keen the kindling sod,
Was not so soft and warm and sweet.

Their pilgrimage's period
A few swift moons have seen complete
Since mother's hands first clasped and shod
    The little feet.

The little hands that never sought
Earth's prizes, worthless all as sands,
What gift has death, God's servant, brought
   The little hands?

We ask: but love's self silent stands,
Love, that lends eyes and wings to thought
To search where death's dim heaven expands.

Ere this, perchance, though love know nought,
Flowers fill them, grown in lovelier lands,
Where hands of guiding angels caught
   The little hands.

The little eyes that never knew
Light other than of dawning skies,
What new life now lights up anew
   The little eyes?

Who knows but on their sleep may rise
Such light as never heaven let through
To lighten earth from Paradise?

No storm, we know, may change the blue
Soft heaven that haply death descries
No tears, like these in ours, bedew
   The little eyes.

Was life so strange, so sad the sky,
　　So strait the wide world's range,
He would not stay to wonder why
　　Was life so strange?

Was earth's fair house a joyless grange
　　Beside that house on high
Whence Time that bore him failed to estrange?

That here at once his soul put by
　　All gifts of time and change,
And left us heavier hearts to sigh
　　'Was life so strange?'

Angel by name love called him, seeing so fair
　　The sweet small frame;
Meet to be called, if ever man's child were,
　　Angel by name.

Rose-bright and warm from heaven's own heart he came,
　　And might not bear
The cloud that covers earth's wan face with shame.

His little light of life was all too rare
　　And soft a flame:
Heaven yearned for him till angels hailed him there
　　Angel by name.

Algernon Charles Swinburne (1837–1909)

Song

All suddenly the wind comes soft,
And Spring is here again;
And the hawthorn quickens with buds of green,
And my heart with buds of pain.

My heart all Winter lay so numb,
The earth so dead and frore,
That I never thought the Spring would come,
Or my heart wake any more.

But Winter's broken and earth has woken,
And the small birds cry again;
And the hawthorn hedge puts forth its buds,
And my heart puts forth its pain.

Rupert Brooke (1887–1915)

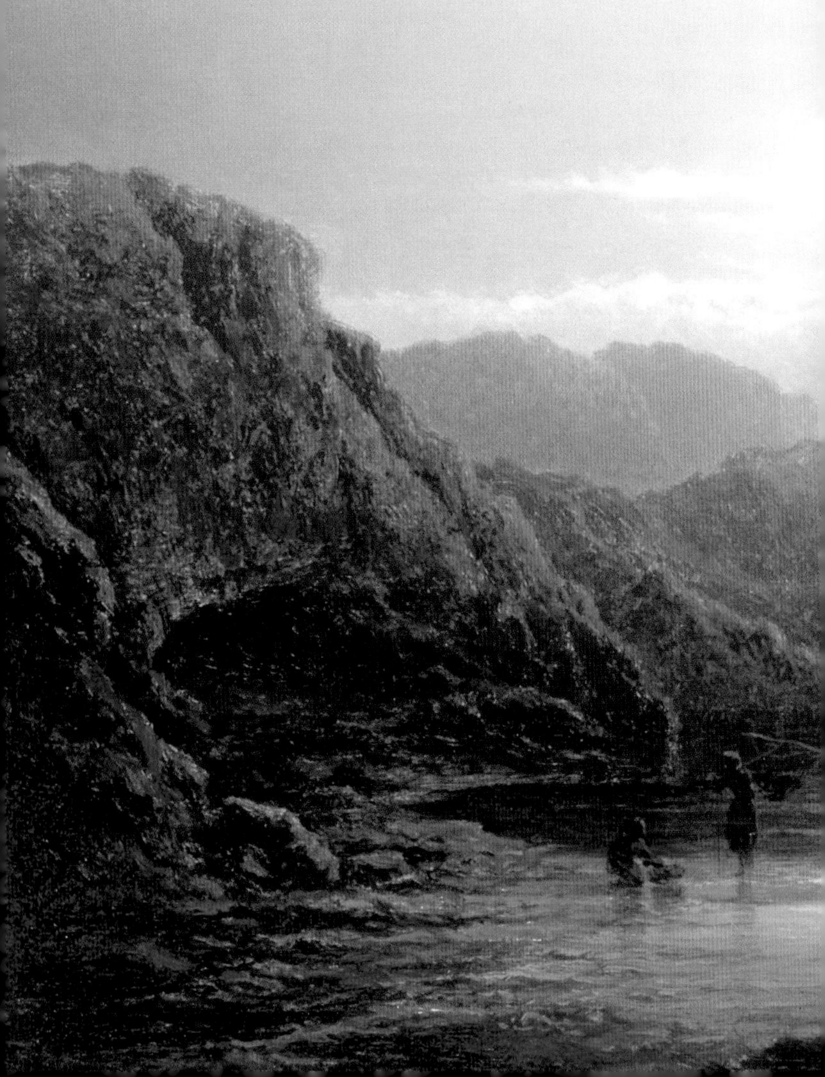

If Death is Kind

Perhaps if Death is kind, and there can be returning,
We will come back to earth some fragrant night,
And take these lanes to find the sea, and bending
Breathe the same honeysuckle, low and white.

We will come down at night to these resounding beaches
And the long gentle thunder of the sea,
Here for a single hour in the wide starlight
We shall be happy, for the dead are free.

Sara Teasdale (1884–1933)

I Meant To Find Her When I Came

I MEANT to find her when I came;
    Death had the same design;
But the success was his, it seems,
    And the discomfit mine.

I meant to tell her how I longed
    For just this single time;
But Death had told her so the first,
    And she had hearkened him.

To wander now is my abode;
    To rest, – to rest would be
A privilege of hurricane
    To memory and me.

Emily Dickinson (1830–86)

A Departed Friend

He is sleeping, sounding sleeping
    In the cold and silent tomb.
He is resting, sweetly resting
    In perfect peace, all alone.

He has left us, God bereft us,
    And his will must e'er be done,
It will grieve us, and bereave us
    To think of this noble son.

While on earth he done his duty,
    To all his fellow men,
Some will miss him in his office,
    Where he often used the pen.

He was witty, always happy,
    Kind and genial in his way;
He was generous in his actions,
    And his honor could display.

He has held many an office,
    And has done his duty well;
And his name will be remembered
    By the friends that knew him well.

Friends are weeping, softly weeping,
In his kind and loving home;
Let him slumber, sweetly slumber,
Till God calls him from the tomb.

Julia A. Moore (1847–1920)

Farewell

Farewell to thee! but not farewell
To all my fondest thoughts of thee:
Within my heart they still shall dwell;
And they shall cheer and comfort me.
O, beautiful, and full of grace!
If thou hadst never met mine eye,
I had not dreamed a living face
Could fancied charms so far outvie.

If I may ne'er behold again
That form and face so dear to me,
Nor hear thy voice, still would I fain
Preserve, for aye, their memory.

That voice, the magic of whose tone
Can wake an echo in my breast,
Creating feelings that, alone,
Can make my tranced spirit blest.

That laughing eye, whose sunny beam
My memory would not cherish less; –
And oh, that smile! whose joyous gleam
Nor mortal language can express.

Adieu, but let me cherish, still,
The hope with which I cannot part.
Contempt may wound, and coldness chill,
But still it lingers in my heart.

And who can tell but Heaven, at last,
May answer all my thousand prayers,
And bid the future pay the past
With joy for anguish, smiles for tears?

Anne Brontë (1820–49)

Death is Nothing at All

Death is nothing at all.
I have only slipped away to the next room.
I am I and you are you.
Whatever we were to each other,
that, we still are.

Call me by my old familiar name.
Speak to me in the easy way
which you always used.
Put no difference into your tone.
Wear no forced air of solemnity or sorrow.

Laugh as we always laughed
at the little jokes we enjoyed together.
Play, smile, think of me. Pray for me.
Let my name be ever the household word
that it always was.
Let it be spoken without effect.
Without the trace of a shadow on it.

Life means all that it ever meant.
It is the same that it ever was.
There is absolute unbroken continuity.
Why should I be out of mind
because I am out of sight?

I am but waiting for you.
For an interval.
Somewhere. Very near.
Just around the corner.

All is well.

Henry Scott-Holland (1847–1918)

Bereavement

I.
How stern are the woes of the desolate mourner
As he bends in still grief o'er the hallowed bier,
As enanguished he turns from the laugh of the scorner,
And drops to perfection's remembrance a tear;
When floods of despair down his pale cheeks are streaming,
When no blissful hope on his bosom is beaming,
Or, if lulled for a while, soon he starts from his dreaming,
And finds torn the soft ties to affection so dear.

II.
Ah! when shall day dawn on the night of the grave,
Or summer succeed to the winter of death?
Rest awhile, hapless victim! and Heaven will save
The spirit that hath faded away with the breath.
Eternity points, in its amaranth bower
Where no clouds of fate o'er the sweet prospect lour,
Unspeakable pleasure, of goodness the dower,
When woe fades away like the mist of the heath.

Percy Bysshe Shelley (1792–1822)

When You Are Old

When you are old and grey and full of sleep,
And nodding by the fire, take down this book,
And slowly read, and dream of the soft look
Your eyes had once, and of their shadows deep;

How many loved your moments of glad grace,
And loved your beauty with love false or true,
But one man loved the pilgrim Soul in you,
And loved the sorrows of your changing face;

And bending down beside the glowing bars,
Murmur, a little sadly, how Love fled
And paced upon the mountains overhead
And hid his face amid a crowd of stars.

W.B. Yeats (1865–1939)

Love In A Life

I.
Room after room,
I hunt the house through
We inhabit together.
Heart, fear nothing, for, heart, thou shalt find her –
Next time, herself! – not the trouble behind her
Left in the curtain, the couch's perfume!
As she brushed it, the cornice-wreath blossomed anew:
Yon looking-glass gleamed at the wave of her feather.

II.
Yet the day wears,
And door succeeds door;
I try the fresh fortune –
Range the wide house from the wing to the centre.
Still the same chance! She goes out as I enter.
Spend my whole day in the quest, – who cares?
But 'tis twilight, you see, – with such suites to explore,
Such closets to search, such alcoves to importune!

Robert Browning (1812–89)

Memorials

Death sets a thing significant
The eye had hurried by,
Except a perished creature
Entreat us tenderly

To ponder little workmanships
In crayon or in wool,
With 'This was last her fingers did,'
Industrious until

The thimble weighed too heavy,
The stitches stopped themselves,
And then 't was put among the dust
Upon the closet shelves.

A book I have, a friend gave,
Whose pencil, here and there,
Had notched the place that pleased him, –
At rest his fingers are.

Now, when I read, I read not,
For interrupting tears
Obliterate the etchings
Too costly for repairs.

Emily Dickinson (1830–86)

A Dream Within A Dream

Take this kiss upon the brow!
And, in parting from you now,
Thus much let me avow –
You are not wrong, who deem
That my days have been a dream;
Yet if hope has flown away
In a night, or in a day,
In a vision, or in none,
Is it therefore the less gone?
All that we see or seem
Is but a dream within a dream.

I stand amid the roar
Of a surf-tormented shore,
And I hold within my hand
Grains of the golden sand –
How few! yet how they creep
Through my fingers to the deep,
While I weep, while I weep!
O God! can I not grasp
Them with a tighter clasp?
O God! can I not save
One from the pitiless wave?
Is all that we see or seem
But a dream within a dream?

Edgar Allan Poe (1809–49)

A Dream

My dead love came to me, and said:
'God gives me one hour's rest,
To spend with thee on earth again:
How shall we spend it best?'

'Why, as of old,' I said; and so
We quarrelled, as of old:
But, when I turned to make my peace,
That one short hour was told.

Stephen Phillips (1864–1915)

Away with Funeral Music

AWAY with funeral music – set
The pipe to powerful lips –
The cup of life's for him that drinks
And not for him that sips.

Robert Louis Stevenson (1850–94)

The Chariot

Because I could not stop for Death,
He kindly stopped for me;
The carriage held but just ourselves
And Immortality.

We slowly drove, he knew no haste,
And I had put away
My labor, and my leisure too,
For his civility.

We passed the school where children played,
Their lessons scarcely done;
We passed the fields of gazing grain,
We passed the setting sun.

We paused before a house that seemed
A swelling of the ground;
The roof was scarcely visible,
The cornice but a mound.

Since then 't is centuries; but each
Feels shorter than the day
I first surmised the horses' heads
Were toward eternity.

Emily Dickinson (1830–86)

My Mother's Memory

There is one bright star in heaven
    Ever shining in my night;
God to me one guide has given
    Like the sailor's beacon light,
Set on every shoal of danger
    Sending out its warning ray
To the homebound weary stranger
    Looking for the land-locked bay.
In my farthest, wildest wand'rings
    I have turned me to that love,
As a diver, 'neath the water,
    Turns to watch the light above.

John Boyle O'Reilly (1844–90)

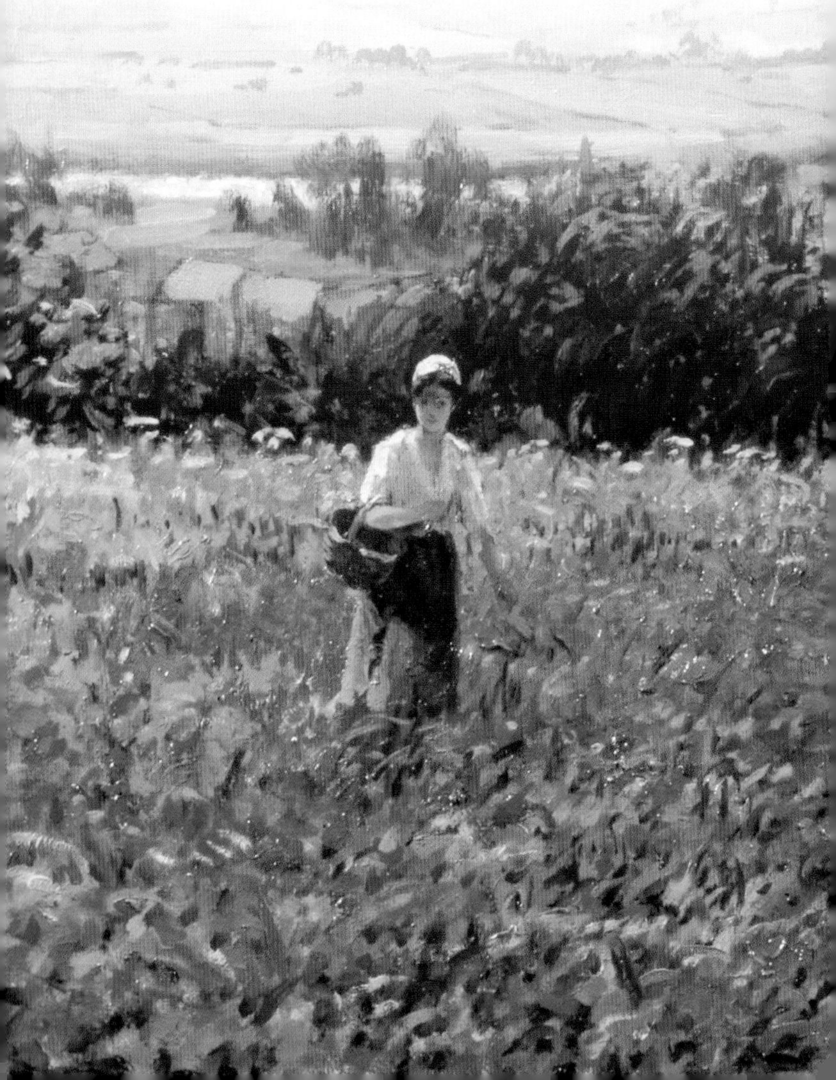

On the Death of a Sister

Dear to my soul! ah, early lost!
Affection's arm was weak to save:
Now friendship's pride, and virtue's boast,
Have come to an untimely grave!

Closed, ever closed, those speaking eyes,
Where sweetness beam'd, where candour shone;
And silent that heart-thrilling voice,
Which music loved, and call'd her own.

That gentle bosom now is cold,
Where feeling's vestal splendours glow'd;
And crumbling down to common mould,
That heart where love and truth abode.

Yet I behold the smile unfeign'd,
Which doubt dispell'd and kindness won;
Yet the soft diffidence, that gain'd
The triumph it appear'd to shun.

Delusion all – forbear, my heart;
These unavailing throbs restrain,
Destruction has perform'd his part,
And Death proclaim'd – thy pangs are vain.

Vain though they be, this heart must swell
With grief that time shall ne'er efface;
And still with bitter pleasure dwell
On ev'ry virtue, ev'ry grace.

For ever lost – I vainly dream'd
That Heaven my early friend would spare;
And, darker as the prospect seem'd,
The more I struggled with despair.

I said – yet a presaging tear
Unbidden rose, and spoke more true –
'She still shall live – th' unfolding year
Shall banish care, and health renew.

'She yet shall tread the flow'ry field,
And catch the opening rose's breath:
To watchful love disease shall yield,
And friendship ward the shaft of death.'

'Alas! before the violet bloom'd –
Before the snows of winter fled;
Too certain fate my hopes consumed,
For she was number'd with the dead.

She died – deserving to be mourn'd,
While parted worth a pang can give.
She died – by Heaven's best gifts adorn'd,
While folly, falsehood, baseness, live.

Long in their baseness live secure
The noxious weed and wounding thorn,
While, snatch'd by violence, ere mature,
The lily from her stem is torn.

Yet who shall blame the heart that feels
When Heaven resumes the good it gave?
Yet who shall scorn the tear that falls
From friendship's eye at virtue's grave?

Friend, parent, sister – tenderest names!
May I, as pale at mem'ry's shrine
Ye pour the tribute anguish claims,
Approach unblamed, and mingle mine.

Long on the joys of vanish'd years
The glance of sadness shall ye cast;
Long, long th' emphatic speech of tears
Shall mourn thy bloom for ever past.

And thou, who from the orient day
Return'st with hope's gay dreams elate,
Falsely secure and vainly gay,
Unconscious of the stroke of fate.

What waits thee? not th' approving smile
Of faithful love that chases care;
Not the fond glance o'er paying toil,
But cold and comfortless despair.

Despair! – I see the phantom rove
On Cail's green banks, no longer bright,
And fiercely grasp the torch of love,
And plunge it in sepulchral night.

Farewell, sweet maiden; at thy tomb
My silent footstep oft shall stray;
More dear to me its hallow'd gloom,
Than life's broad glare, and fortune's day.

And oft, as fancy paints thy bier,
And mournful eyes thy lowly bed,
The secret sigh shall rise – the tear
That shuns observance shall be shed.

Nor shall the thoughts of thee depart,
Nor shall my soul regret resign,
Till mem'ry perish, till this heart
Be cold and motionless as thine.

James Grahame (1765–1811)

Goodbye, My Friend, Goodbye

Goodbye, my friend, goodbye
My love, you are in my heart.
It was preordained we should part
And be reunited by and by.
Goodbye: no handshake to endure.
Let's have no sadness – furrowed brow.
There's nothing new in dying now
Though living is no newer.

Sergei Aleksandrovich Esenin (1895–1925)

Sweetheart, Good-bye

SWEETHEART, good-bye! Our varied day
Is closing into twilight gray,
And up from bare, bleak wastes of sea
The north-wind rises mournfully;
A solemn prescience, strangely drear,
Doth haunt the shuddering twilight air;
It fills the earth, it chills the sky –
Sweetheart, good-bye!

Sweetheart, good-bye! Our joys are passed,
And night with silence comes at last;
All things must end, yea, – even love –
Nor know we, if reborn above,
The heart-blooms of our earthly prime
Shall flower beyond these bounds of time.
'Ah! death alone is sure!' we cry –
Sweetheart, good-bye!

Sweetheart, good-bye! Through mists and tears
Pass the pale phantoms of our years,
Once bright with spring, or subtly strong
When summer's noontide thrilled with song;
Now wan, wild-eyed, forlornly bowed,
Each rayless as an autumn cloud
Fading on dull September's sky –
Sweetheart, good-bye!

Sweetheart, good-bye! The vapors rolled
Athwart, you distant, darkening wold
Are types of what our world doth know
Of tenderest loves of long ago;
And thus, when all is done and said,
Our life lived out, our passion dead,
What can their wavering record be
But tinted mists of memory?
Oh! clasp and kiss me ere we die –
Sweetheart, good-bye!

Paul Hamilton (1830–87)

To One Departed

Seraph! thy memory is to me
Like some enchanted far-off isle
In some tumultuous sea –
Some ocean vexed as it may be
With storms; but where, meanwhile,
Serenest skies continually
Just o'er that one bright island smile.
For 'mid the earnest cares and woes
That crowd around my earthly path,
(Sad path, alas, where grows
Not even one lonely rose!)
My soul at least a solace hath
In dreams of thee; and therein knows
An Eden of bland repose.

Edgar Allan Poe (1809–49)

Picture Credits

All images are courtesy of Fine Art Photographic Library

Index of Titles

Index of Poets